Millennium Memories

The History of Gorsley & Kilcot

Millennium Memories

The History of Gorsley & Kilcot

Edited by
Lee Hines

Gorsley & Kilcot Millennium Committee
in association with
Logaston Press

GORSLEY & KILCOT MILLENNIUM COMMITTEE
Secretary: Kilcot House, Kilcot,
Gloucestershire GL18 1NQ

LOGASTON PRESS
Little Logaston, Woonton, Almeley,
Herefordshire HR3 6QH

First published by Logaston Press 2001

ISBN 1 873827 82 2

Set in Times and Baskerville by Logaston Press
and printed in Great Britain by
The Cromwell Press

Contents

FOREWORD

The idea for a book on the history of Gorsley and Kilcot first arose from the meetings of the Millennium Committee. As well as the 'Fun Day' celebration and commemorative mugs for the children it was felt that something more permanent was needed and it was agreed that some form of historical record would be appropriate.

The original concept was a mainly pictorial record of the last century with reminiscences from current and previous residents. But, like Topsy, 'it growed'—chiefly due to the wealth of material which was made available.

Although the major part of the book still deals with the last hundred years or so, it has been put into historical context with a brief description of the area's past from pre-Roman times. It also looks to the future by including the views of current residents—especially the younger ones—and the results of the Gorsley and Kilcot parish appraisal, carried out in February 2001.

Our grateful thanks are due to all who contributed towards this book, and especially to Eileen Chivers for a major input into the research at the beginning of the project, and to Lee Hines who, through her expertise, has made the book a reality.

One of the benefits of the Millennium Committee's work has been to bring together a community artificially divided by bureaucracy. With the aid of a grant from the Lottery Heritage Initiative Fund this book is but the first of a series of activities which it is hoped will reinforce this revived sense of community.

Revd Robert Simpson
Chairman
Gorsley & Kilcot Millennium Committee

ACKNOWLEDGMENTS

It would have been impossible to produce this book without the willing help and co-operation of so many people who gave unsparingly of their time, delved into memories, opened photo albums and scrapbooks, spent hours in the library or on the internet. To them all, a very big Thank You.

The grant which made the project viable came through the Local Heritage Initiative, funded by the Heritage Lottery Fund and Nationwide Building Society and administered by the Countryside Agency: to all of whom our thanks are particularly due.

Thanks are also due to the helpful and patient staff at the Gloucestershire Records Office, Gloucester City Museum, Ross Library and Herefordshire Records Office for answering queries from various researchers and to Gorsley & Kilcot Parish Council and Linton Parish Council for their unwavering support. The staff of the *Ross Gazette* were more than helpful when checking dates and going through back issues.

Without the work of the Gorsley and Kilcot Millennium Committee under its chairman, Revd Robert Simpson, and secretary, Vivien Ferguson, the whole idea for a book would never have been conceived. Especial thanks are due to Eileen Chivers who acted as 'midwife' to the book, to Dr Anne Clough for additional research and to John Wheble for invaluable help with photographs. Martin Davy read the proofs and gently pointed out the errors. My fellow members of the book sub-committee, Julie Buckley, Gloria Pay, and Judy Sleet, were untiring in their support.

But the greatest debt is owed to all those past and present residents who helped with reminiscences, information, photos and above all, gave their time towards recording this history. They include: Les Aubrey, Peter Atkinson, Tony Beckwith, Fred Bach, Lydia Buckley, Sean Burkill, Stephen Burson, Revd Roy Chivers, Maureen Chlupac (of Healesville, Australia), Dr Cecil Clough, Mrs F.

Coleman, Christine Crowhurst, James Crowhurst, Mary Davies (née Phillips), Olive Davis, Tony Davis, Sarah Ferguson, Mrs Fluck, Hubert Gooch, Norman Gooch, Winston Gooch, Revd Patrick and Beryl Goodland, Ruby Goulding, Sarah Hamblin, Erie Hayward, Esther Howley, Frank Huggins, Joyce Johnson, Neil Maddocks, Frankie Martin, Ida Martin, Andrew McIntosh, Ron Mogg, David Plowman, Dora Powell (née Fishpool), Amanda Price, Topsie Price, Graham Price, Lesley Rackley, Mary Smith, Kathleen Spragg, Elizabeth Taylor, Geoff Taylor, Venice Watkins, Gerald Yeates.

Thanks are also due to: Donald Pennington, Peter Hill and Pauline Wood of Linton & District History Society for generous help with research and illustrations; the Secretary and staff of Ross-on-Wye Golf Club for information and the photograph of A.D. Evans; Michael Orr for assistance in tracing the details of those who died in the First and Second World Wars; Mrs Robbie Hazan of St Dunstan's and Keith Hills-Trahearne of Trahearne Portraits for permission to use the school photograph. A special thank you to Clive Westall, head teacher, the staff and pupils of Gorsley Goffs School, and in particular the children of Year 6 in 2000 and 2001.

Without the advice, help and expertise of Andy Johnson of Logaston Press this book could never have been published. His enthusiasm for local history has been an inspiration for many of us over the years.

Last, but never least, I must thank my husband, Peter Hines, for his patience and good humour while this project took over our home.

The constraints of time, space and finance have meant that not all material could be used and apologies are sincerely offered for these omissions and also for any errors which have occurred in the journey from memory to the printed page.

L. H.
Kilcot, September 2001

CHAPTER I
Before Domesday

Pre-Roman

More than 2,000 years ago—before the birth of Christ and before the Romans came to Britain—it is more than likely that people were living in this area. Although there are no known or excavated sites of pre-Roman buildings in Kilcot and Gorsley, there are the remains of a hill fort on Chase Hill on the outskirts of Ross and flints, axe-heads and similar items have been turned up in fields and gardens in the surrounding area. Examples of these are on show in Newent's Market Hall.

From these small, everyday items we can tell that people lived here who traded with folk from other parts of England and Wales, as the geology of some of the stone artefacts is not local. Pre-Roman Britain, far from being a barbaric wilderness, was an ordered, tribal society, with established trading routes both within its bounds and overseas. Although most of the country was forested, agriculture had ensured that large tracts were cleared, especially in the southern and more lowland areas of England and eastern Wales.

Roman

The Roman occupation of Britain started in the south-east and spread steadily north and west, reaching just beyond the modern boundaries of Wales and Scotland. We know that the Romans were active in this area, primarily for iron ore. A major iron smelting site (*Ariconium*) near Bromsash ranked alongside mines in the Forest of Dean for importance. Roads were built to join *Ariconium*, Mitcheldean, Lydney and Gloucester. Gloucester itself (Roman

1

Glevum) was one of the five most important towns in Roman Britain. Its civic authority covered the surrounding countryside.

As the years went by, the Roman occupation mellowed in its militaristic ferocity—at least away from the borderlands. More Roman soldiers and administrators stayed in England when their service time had expired and intermarriage became more common. Settlements expanded and, like many a retired soldier or civil servant, the Romans had their own 'little place in the country'. Evidence of this is widespread, but perhaps the most surprising is that when the M50 was being constructed, archaeologists found, on average, five Roman villas in every mile of motorway.

Tombstone of Roman cavalryman, 1st century AD, in Gloucester City Museum

The Saxons and the Kingdom of Mercia

The Roman Empire began to dissolve in the fifth century as problems nearer home caused the Romans to loose their grip on far-flung colonies such as Britain. The way was open for invasion by the peoples of northern Germany and Scandinavia—the Angles, Saxons and Jutes. Many of the existing inhabitants fled westwards, across the Severn and the Wye into the Welsh mountains, where they retained their Celtic lifestyle, and some Roman practices, including

Christianity which had become the 'official' religion in the fourth century.

The border between the new Saxon kingdoms of Britain and the older Celtic tribelands was marked most spectacularly in this area by

The Saxon cross in St Mary's Church, Newent

the building of Offa's Dyke. Offa, the Anglo-Saxon King of Mercia, had this vast defensive earthwork built in about AD 784, by which time England and much of the Welsh and Scottish border country had been divided into separate kingdoms by the invaders following two centuries of conflict.

Gradually, as life became more peaceful, Saxon communities became established and it is from this era that 'the village' first appears in a form that we recognise today. The Saxon village was a rural community, with houses grouped close together and strip-fields around them which were used for arable agriculture, while other areas were common land (*i.e.* land held in common) for animal pasture. The villagers owed allegiance to a local lord (thane) and paid rent in goods or service. In return he offered protection against human and animal raiders.

Christianity returned to Britain with the arrival of St

3

Augustine in Kent and St Aidan in Northumbria allied with the missionary zeal of Theodore of Tarsus, Archbishop of Canterbury, towards the end of the seventh century. Over the next two hundred years many churches were founded on the sites where successor churches stand today. Indeed, part of a ninth-century Saxon cross was found in Newent churchyard indicating that worship has been continuous here for more than a millennium.

Despite the many wars of succession, which were finally decided in 1066, it was a generally peaceful and settled society which William of Normandy claimed. However, it was divided into many competing feudal lordships and William, anxious to know exactly what he had gained by the conquest—and more to the point, how much tax he could raise and what lands he could reward his knights with— ordered that an assessment be made. The decree was made in 1085 at his Christmas Court in Gloucester. The result was the Domesday Book.

CHAPTER II
Domesday and After

There is no separate entry for Gorsley in the *Domesday Book,* but Kilcot is mentioned under the spelling Chilecot:

> Chilecot
> Land of Ansfrid de Cormeilles. In Botloe Hundred. Pauntley $1^1/_2$ hides, Kilcot 1 hide, Ketford, 1 hide, Hayes 1 hide. Total $4^1/_2$ hides. Wulfheln, Alfward and Wiga held them as four manors. $1^1/_2$ hides are free from tax. In Lordship 2 ploughs. 7 villagers and 3 smallholders with 7 ploughs. 2 slaves. A mill at 7s 6d. The value was £3 10s, now £4. The holders of these lands could go where they would.

From this we learn that Kilcot was part of a larger landholding, the hundred of Botloe and it now belonged to Ansfrid, the Abbot of Cormeilles. The 'hide' was an area used for tax assessment and is thought to have been about 120 acres. Originally the land belonged to three Saxon lords and comprised four manorial holdings. Part of this was free of tax.

Two areas of land (enough to be covered by a plough team of eight oxen) were worked by the sub-tenant himself. Additionally there were seven other ox-plough areas which were used by villagers (a well-off peasant with quite a lot of land) and smallholders (a middle class of peasant with not so much land). There were also two slaves or landless peasants.

The mill paid 7s 6d (37.5p) tax. The total tax bill had been £3 10 shillings (£3.50) but was now £4. The chief tenants could transfer the lands without reference to a higher authority.

The Royal Forest of Dean

At the time of Domesday about a quarter of the land surveyed was owned by the church. The Abbey of Cormeilles also owned Newent and Aston Ingham, while Ross was part of the lands of Hereford Church and Lea belonged to Gloucester Church. All these settlements were on the edge of the Royal Forest of Dean and it was the Normans, with their love of hunting, who decreed the Forest to be subject to special laws. These laws were very harsh on the ordinary peasant who wanted to collect firewood, graze his animals or supplement his diet with a bit of wild boar or venison. Special courts were set up to deal with those who broke the forest laws and the boundaries of the Forest of Dean increased in the century following Domesday to include Gorsley and Kilcot in its jurisdiction.

Of the many surveys made to ascertain the boundaries, that of 1228 is recorded and it follows the boundaries already asserted to have been 'before 1154':

> From the bridge on the west of Gloucester, along the great road to Newent, thence by the same road to the stream of Gorsley, thence ascending that stream to its source, then by a road to Bromsash, thence descending by the same road to Alton, thence by the same road to the Wye ...

The next time the forest limits were surveyed was in 1282 when a special court or 'eyre' was held. Everyone living within the forest could be summoned and we learn that Bogo de Knovile was fined half a mark (about 33p) for the 'wasting' or despoiling of his wood at Kilcot. At that time the limits of the Forest of Dean were described as:

> ... by the stream of Alton as far as the public way coming from Ross as far as the oak outside Weston. And so by the King's highway beyond the bridge as far as a certain tree called Bolletree. And thus by the King's highway as far as the millpond of Buriton which is Richard Talbot's. And thus by the King's highway up to a certain cross called Luce Cross. And thus by the King's highway through the middle of Gorsley as far as Gorsley Ford. And thus going down by the brook as far as Oxenhall bridge. And thus by the King's highway as far as the prior of Newent's bridge ...

Although within the Forest of Dean for purposes of law, this did not mean that Kilcot and Gorsley were entirely wooded. Indeed, the gradual deforestation of the area was to be a continuing concern of the Crown over the next five hundred years. But for the ordinary inhabitants the clearing of land for more agriculture was a welcome change. Other events were less welcome.

Death and Destruction

In 1348 the plague arrived in south-west England. Known as The Black Death, because of the dark swellings which characterised the illness, it spread through Dorset and Somerset, enveloped Bristol and made its way up the Severn to Gloucester.

While there are no records to show how badly it affected Gorsley and Kilcot, there is no reason to believe that it did not strike down between one third and one half of the population—the general mortality rate. It is difficult for us today to imagine the terror which this disease wrought not only because of its high fatality rate, but also because in those days people believed that it was a judgement on them from God for being sinful. Their terror was made all the worse when, priests being struck down as much, if not more, than laymen, there were no clergy to hear their confessions and administer the last rites, thereby imperilling the immortal soul.

We do know, from the Bishop of Hereford's records, that one of the earliest fatalities, in the spring of 1349, was the parish priest of St Mary's, Linton, but a successor was soon appointed. The general locality may have been particularly badly hit by the plague, for the records show that within the space of six months in 1349 no fewer than three vicars were appointed to Ross.

The long-term effect of the Black Death was to depopulate and destabilise the countryside as people moved to find work, food and shelter.

Further destabilisation arose in the following century with the long drawn-out Wars of the Roses, with the houses of York and Lancaster disputing the Crown. One of the most bloody and decisive battles of these wars was at Tewkesbury in 1471 and it is hard to conceive that our villagers were not affected either directly in the fighting or by the aftermath, with armed men wandering the countryside looking for refuge.

Despite all this death and destruction, there are indications that the standard of living was improving. Newent had been granted the right to hold a weekly market in 1253 together with two annual fairs and this helped the prosperity of the town, which was further improved in Tudor times as the wool trade expanded. Local Ryeland sheep gave their name to the area round the market town, which also expanded beyond agriculture with the opening of the glassworks in 1600, a cloth mill in 1608 and iron works in 1639.

As well as iron, coal was mined in the area and in 1608 one John Hodges of Kilcot was described as 'a coleminer'. How extensive the workings were at that time we do not know, but in 1795 mining started in earnest in the area between Kilcot Hill and the Oxenhall road (see below) around Hill House Farm, White House and Lower House.

During the Siege of Gloucester in the Civil War (1643) miners from the Forest of Dean were employed by the Royalists to undermine the defences of the city. On the restoration of the monarchy Charles II enjoyed hunting in the Dean and began to restore the depredations which had been made. However, by now the limits of the Royal Forest were severely curtailed and did not reach beyond the present Gloucester/Ross road.

By the beginning of the eighteenth century the Manor of Kilcot (the estate rather than a building) was acquired, through marriage, by Walter Nourse, a well-known local dignitary. We have a description of the area in 1712 from Sir Robert Atkyns' *Ancient and Present State of Gloucestershire.*

> There are several good houses in this Parish belonging to John Bourne, Esq., Mr Thomas Stoackes, Mr Stephen Skinner, Mr Miles Beale, Mr Thomas Maltster and Mr Richard Paulton, who have all good estates in this place.
>
> There was heretofore a chapel near Corsley [*sic*] Common dedicated to St Hilary and St Elias but it is now wholly demolished. The site is recognisable under the name of St Hillys Nap or Tump and the field lies on the NW side of Kilcot Hill.
>
> Kilcot means the cell of the wood and hermit missionaries building a small cell or oratory of wattles summoned to devotion those who liked to resort thither to hear and pray.

The site of St Hilary's Chapel is still recorded by the field name 'Chapel Meadow' on Kilcot Hill. Sir Robert uses the present-day spelling of Kilcot, but until the middle of the twentieth century it was usually spelled Kilcote. Gorsley was originally Gorstleye (gorse-field), by 1725 Gorstley Common was recorded and in the nineteenth century the village became Gorsley.

Road and Rail

Sir Robert Atkyns did not mention the state of the local roads, but most commentators in the early eighteenth century found fault with them. The difficulties of transport had served to keep Gorsley and Kilcot, like many other communities, isolated from all but the most everyday happenings. But at the turn of the century life began to change, first with the opening of the Hereford and Gloucester Canal in 1795 and then the completion of a new turnpike road in 1810. Newent and Ross, Gloucester and Hereford—and the wider world beyond—all became more accessible.

Raising money for road repairs through the payment of tolls had begun at the beginning of the century and had been extended to the major routes from Gloucester by 1726. But these toll or turnpike roads were not always well kept and people resented paying for poor roads. In May 1734 an armed mob destroyed the city gates and then ran through Gloucester shouting 'Blood for Blood' and 'Down with the Turnpikes'.

These roads ran along routes we would recognise today. The present A40 follows much the same way as the former Ross-Gloucester turnpike. Other routes were from Gloucester to Ledbury via Newent and to Monmouth by way of the 'new road' through Mitcheldean and Coleford (now the A4136). None of these turnpike roads passed through Kilcot or Gorsley until the early nineteenth century when under the terms of the 1802 Newent Road Act three new roads were proposed.

The first went through the 'several parishes of Newent, Linton and Upton Bishop to join the [Hereford]... Turnpike Road at a place called The Crows Hill'. This is the road now denoted as the B4221 between Newent and Upton Bishop. The other two roads were:

> ... the road leading from the bottom of Kilcott Hill near a place called Phillip's Cottage ... to the Lea Line ... and also the road branching out of the said last road near a place called Perrin's Wood in the parish of Aston Ingham ... and passing

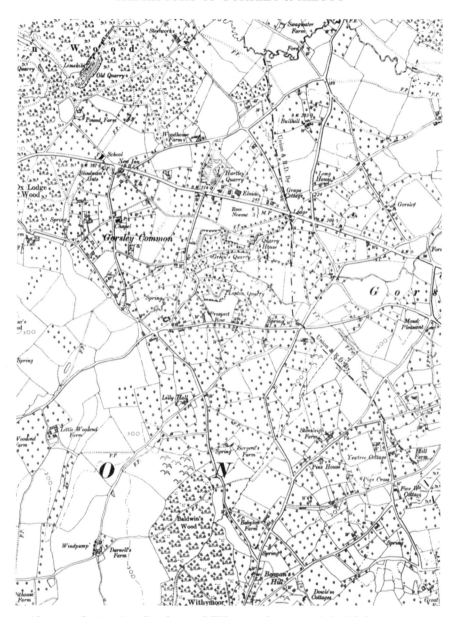

Above and opposite: Gorsley and Kilcot at the turn of the 18th century—
OS maps published in 1903 and 1905

through a place called the Croose Green and joining the road
leading from ... Newent to ... Hereford, near the Great Pool on
Gorsley Common ...

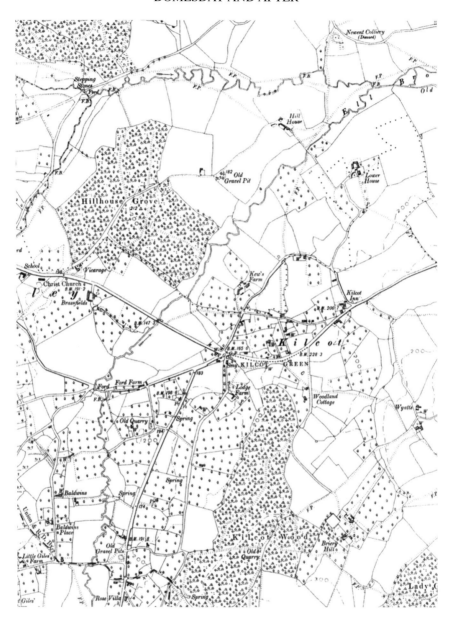

The first of these is now the B4222 from Kilcot Cross to Lea via Aston
Ingham and Aston Crews. The second is the minor road from Aston
Crews down Beavan's Hill to Linton Hall and the road to Kempley.
Until these roads were completed, in 1810, the only routes through

11

the area were muddy tracks, rutted in the summer and awash in the winter. The main route to Ross had been via Linton, past Great Woodend Farm and on through Bromsash and Weston.

Canals and Coal

More than a decade before the improvement of the roads, however, the Hereford and Gloucester Canal had reached Newent, affording an easy way to transport goods to Gloucester. The impetus for this had been partly based on the exploitation of the Newent Coalfield, but the mines never reached the hoped-for tonnage, the link to Hereford did not open until 1845 and both projects ended in financial disaster.

Although the main part of the Newent Coalfield was at Boulsdon, shafts were also sunk at Kilcot near Hill House, White House and Lower House Farms. The first coal was mined in 1794 and for a few years enough was produced to be sold as far as Stroud. Most of it is thought to have gone to the limekilns at Green's Quarry, Gorsley. While the White House and Lower House shafts fell into disuse, those at Hill House continued sporadically, with mining definitely being underway at the time of the 1841 census. The coal was never of sufficient quality and quantity to justify great expenditure on its extraction and the lack of coal freight was instrumental in the failure of the Hereford and Gloucester Canal.

Taking the place of the canal—quite literally in some sections—came the railway. In 1885 the Gloucester/Ledbury line opened, the famous 'Daffodil Line' named for the wild daffodils which were picked from the area, especially Kempley and Dymock, and sent to London markets on early morning trains. The nearest manned station was Newent, but there was a halt at Four Oaks, near Oxenhall, where trains would stop on request.

With better road and even rail connections, the farmers and smallholders who made up most of the population had better access to markets. They also came into contact with new ideas and opportunities. Chief among these in Gorsley was the twin development of a school and Baptist Chapel from the 1830s. Education and worship were the cornerstones of the expanding village and this was reflected with a similar development for the Anglican community later in the century.

Chapter III
The Last 100 Years

With the first shots of the Great War in August 1914, life in the community, as in so many others, changed forever. Young men marched off to a war 'that would be over by Christmas'; thousands never returned. In addition to the names listed on the war memorials were those who came home broken in health.

With so many men away, industry and agriculture had to rely on other forms of labour. Women took jobs outside the home for the first time; on the farm, mechanisation replaced the horse and his handler. There were fewer jobs available for the soldiers when they came home and agriculture in general was depressed in the post-war years, with low prices for produce and low wages for the few workers who were needed.

The effect was worst on farms which employed large numbers of labourers. Those with their own family farms or smallholdings and those with certain skills fared better and the improvement in the roads and the railways meant that markets for produce were more easily reached. Children who attended Picklenash School usually had to walk but on their way home, if they timed it properly, they would hitch a lift on the back of a smallholder's cart which had been taking goods to Newent railway station and was also on its way home.

Frank Huggins' father, Percival, came back to the family farm in 1918 after serving abroad. Frank remembers him fetching cattle feed (grains) from the old brewery in Ross with a horse-drawn trolley. On one occasion he was fined for not having a name on the side of the trolley and Frank's sister, Ruby made a metal nameplate. Frank's maternal grandfather, Charlie Pensom, was a basket-maker and

Frank would take his turnip kypes and Gloster pots (square baskets for the fruit sales) to Gloucester market.

Nor was the traffic all one way. Peter Atkinson recalls that in the 1920s one of his relations in Kilcot used to take in washing which had arrived by train from London. The laundry came in big wicker baskets which were delivered by horse and cart. The laundry was in an outhouse with two boilers and shelves all around to house the flat-irons.

Until the 1930s most traffic was horse-drawn, although the postman would come by bicycle. Mary Davies (née Phillips) remembers her mother 'driving the pony and trap to take and fetch passengers from the station at Newent'. An irregular bus service to Gloucester was offered by William Sterry, who put seats in the covered lorry in which he transported cider and perry. A Gorsley resident remembers the first proper bus: 'The first bus to run from Gloucester to Gorsley belonged to Mr Davies. The bus ran once a day, three times a week and each Thursday Mr Davies would run a bus through to Ross'.

The arrival of motor vehicles led to the need for motor mechanics and garages. The garage at Kilcot Cross was thriving in 1936 when, alas, it burnt down. The old wooden structure was replaced by a brick garage in 1938.

Telephones came to Gorsley in the 1930s and the exchange was housed in a room in the then Post Office, owned by Mr and Mrs Aubrey. (In 1962 the Post Office moved to the village shop by the

Motor vehicles became more common in the 1930s.
Kilcot Cross and new garage

Sugar Tump and in 1969, on the retirement of Mr and Mrs Allport, to the Royal Stores, where it is today.) Seven subscribers were needed before lines were installed. The story is told of one school-child, seeing the GPO telegraph poles being erected, asked a workman what the letters GPO stood for. 'Gorsley Pickled Onions' came the reply. Until the telephone arrived if a doctor was needed someone had to walk, cycle or ride to Newent and hope that he was not already out on a call. By 1939 there were more telephones, including public call boxes, and buses ran to Ross and Newent eight times a day in each direction, with additional services to Ross on Thursday (market day).

The coming of the Second World War meant huge changes for the community and this period is dealt with in more detail in a following section. As well as the exodus of men—and women—joining the Armed Forces, there was an influx of evacuee children from London, Liverpool and Birmingham. The Red Cross took over Linton Hall where wounded soldiers were nursed back to health, women went out to work to take the place of the men at the front, and German POWs were put to work in the fields under the watchful eye of old men and schoolboys.

Horse power was still used, especially in the war years. Joyce Johnson (née Sysum) and Betty Fishpool (née Johnson) in the 1940s, having taken the pony and cart to Gloucester market

One of the side-effects of the Second World War was the increase in the number of people—especially women—who learned to drive a car or a truck. In the late 1950s, as prosperity gradually returned, more and more families acquired their own vehicle. Road transport of goods also grew and a defining moment in the history of Gorsley and Kilcot was the opening of the M50 motorway in 1960, with its junction just beyond the school at Jays Green.

The previous decade had seen several changes in the life of the community. Water mains were laid in the late 1950s (and continued to be laid and upgraded over the years) so families were no longer reliant on water from the well. Electricity arrived between 1961 and 1963 (depending on where you lived), which meant farewell to the paraffin lamp, boiling water on the range or—at best—the diesel generator. Houses on the main roads could even be connected to piped gas. And those main roads became busier and busier with traffic. Christine Crowhurst recalls: 'When I first came here (in the early 1980s) I could ride into Newent with a horse and trap and children would ride bikes everywhere. The main road was just a country lane. But it soon became too busy and too dangerous'.

The rise of the motor car began to change the face of the community in other ways, as people who worked in Gloucester, Ross or further afield, moved in. Before the war about 40% of the Gorsley population had been directly employed in agriculture full-time. One in three of the labour force were in the service industries, which included domestic service for many of the women. Fifty years on, by the time of the 1991 census, two-thirds of the local community in employment were in a white-collar job and all commuted by car to their place of work.

But the cost of motoring, in terms of money, accidents and quality of life is now being questioned. In February 2001 a parish appraisal was carried out for the new civil parish of Gorsley and Kilcot (see p.96). Over 80 per cent of residents responded and the area of most concern was roads and transport—too much traffic, the poor state of the roads and the lack of a reliable and inexpensive bus service.

There are other signs that attitudes and lifestyles are changing. There is a general rise in self-employment, and technology has ensured that more people can work from home, or close by. The parish appraisal revealed that 40 per cent of those in work were running their own business and while the majority of these were still in agriculture/horticulture, other occupations were represented including leisure/tourism and professional services like accountancy.

CHAPTER IV

Chapel, Church and School

What is it that binds a community together? It is in part a sharing of experience and memories which, in a formal setting, includes religious worship and education. This was very true in the nineteenth and early twentieth century when folk who had spent their working week in scattered houses would come together on Sunday to worship, and especially to mark the great Christian celebrations of Easter and Christmas. In Victorian times acquaintance would be widened amongst the young through attendance at a village school. As the century turned and life became a little easier, leisure pursuits were followed and the village hall became a focus for activity. But the heart of the village still centred around worship and education.

Worship: The Baptist Chapel

A significant driving force behind the development of Gorsley as a community was the establishment of the Baptist Chapel and Gorsley Goffs School. At the beginning of the nineteenth century visiting preachers from Ryeford ministered to the growing number of Nonconformist worshippers. Pastor John Hall, writing in 1831 about the early days noted:

> The worship at Gorsley was conducted first at a house called the Stillworks; but the congregation increasing this was found too small; and a large room was procured at a house called Blindman's Gate, for which the church at Ryeford, though poor themselves, paid a rent of thirty shillings annually, and where their present Pastor continued to preach till the year

1819. Oftimes in the summer when this large room would not contain the people attending, Mr Williams preached under a tree in the garden ...

The overcrowding and Pastor Williams' other commitments led the congregation to approach the Edward Goff Charity for help. Edward Goff, a farm labourer from Huntington, Herefordshire, had worked his way up in the world to become a wealthy and respected London merchant, known for his piety and charity. He died in 1813 and left his money to promote and establish schools for the education of poor children. Reflecting his beliefs the charity connected the schools with Christian ministry and the usual arrangement was that the schoolmaster would also be the village pastor.

By 1819 Gorsley had its own Baptist minister and schoolmaster and two years later the chapel was built—this is now the older section of the school. The early years of the ministry in Gorsley were fraught with difficulties—the first minister was 'an awfully immoral character' and the second had a disagreement with some members of the congregation—but in 1831 Pastor John Hall came to the village.

John Hall typified so many of the Victorian qualities we admire today. Strong in his beliefs, and physically strong also; a man of tireless energy which he used in the service of others. Coming from humble beginnings he had little formal education himself and believed passionately in the advantages of education, an enthusiasm which found ready acceptance among his flock. Such was the success

Gorsley Goffs School—original home of the Baptist Chapel

Pupils of Gorsley Goffs School enact the story of their founder, Edward Goff, in a musical drama 'The man who made a million', written by Revd Patrick Goodland and performed in July 1994

of his ministry that five years later the congregation had outgrown the new chapel and moved to 'a room capable of accommodating one hundred people' at Blindman's Gate. In 1851, the year of the Great Exhibition, work started on a new building, with all members of the congregation contributing whatever they could in terms of labour, materials or money. The completed chapel, capable of holding 400 people, opened in May 1852.

The untiring work of Pastor Hall and leading members of the congregation was gradually having its effect on 'Heathen's Heath' as Gorsley was commonly known. The name arose from the presence of many who had established squatters rights on Gorsley Common, most of whom would rather not come into contact with the law. Indeed, the story is told of an Assize Court Judge in Gloucester who remarked with surprise that none of the malefactors before him that session had come from Heathen's Heath. This was a slur on the honest folk of the community, who could find it hard to get employment if they gave Gorsley as their address.

But even within the congregation there were wrongdoers as the church minute book reveals:

> 1845 June 18th CD excluded for ill usage of his wife and other acts of immorality.
> 1853 March 9th PP excluded for criminal intercourse with another man, she was detected by her husband; and on his evidence expelled. Her general behaviour to her husband is bad.

John Hall continued as minister until 1881, when ill health forced him to retire. As well as Pastor, he had been headmaster of the school until 1864, had overseen the formation of a lending library and a friendly society to look after the sick and unemployed and had also seen new chapels formed in Kempley and Crow Hill. He died in 1885.

By then the chapel had become the focus of life for many in Gorsley. In addition to worship the congregation would be involved in other activities such as the Harvest Auction and the Sunday School outings, which, it seems, were not always confined to the children of chapel members. 'There was always poor attendance [at the National, *i.e.* C of E, School] when the Baptist Chapel held their Feast Day in June' a former pupil remembers. David Cox, a member of the Chapel, recalls in his memoirs:

20

> The 'treat' took the form of an outing to May Hill by horse-drawn wagonette, an excursion which I remember with keen delight, the rather bumpy journey through winding, leafy lanes jogging slowly along between the hedgerows without a care in the world ...

Mary Davies (née Philips) also remembers those visits to May Hill: 'When we arrived the Sunday School teachers would throw handfuls of sweets for the children to find'.

Pastor Stanley Cox, who came to Gorsley in 1909, helped establish many of these events in the village calendar. An enthusiastic minister, like many of his generation, he felt compelled to serve in the 1914-1918 War, where he tended the injured and dying. And like so many of his generation he returned in 1919 broken in health. He continued his ministry but died a few years later aged only 41.

The post-war years saw the building of a chapel at Kilcot. There was already a temporary structure for the Sunday School just up from Kilcot Cross on the Aston Ingham road and the New Baptist Chapel was built alongside. It was opened in June 1934 by T. Lindsey Price, treasurer of the Baptist Association, with the Minister, Revd H. Roderick, but closed some sixty years later and the congregation transferred to Gorsley. The building is now a private house.

The war changed life irrevocably, especially in rural communities. Those young men who returned did not want to go back to agricultural labour with its long hours and poor pay. And mechanisation meant that farmers could do without many of their workers. Mechanisation also meant travel by bus, instead of horse and cart, opening up new horizons. The Revd Patrick Goodland, Pastor from 1976 to 1994, describes these changes in his *Gorsley Chapel Story*:

> The carriers' cart gave way to Bayliss' Bus Services which in turn was swallowed up by the Red and White Bus Services running from Monmouth to Gloucester via Ross, Gorsley and Newent. The village blacksmith was trying to adapt to being a motor mechanic. Some of the brighter sparks among the young men were striving to fathom the miraculous workings of the petrol driven electric dynamo, which could provide domestic lighting.

The Baptist Chapel today

Mains electricity was not to come to the village until 1961 and some places as late as 1963. The post-war decades of the 1950s and 1960s was the most rapid period of change in Gorsley and Kilcot with the introduction of electricity, mains water and the opening of the M50. Wartime had again broadened the horizons of many villagers; increased leisure time and an overall improved standard of living together with the memories of war saw a crisis of faith among many and sharply dropping church attendances. Weekly worship was no longer the centre of village life.

And then the pendulum swung back. Better communication brought an influx of newcomers to the village; interest in spiritual matters grew and the Chapel began to host events like the Flower Festival (started in 1980) which has now grown beyond the community into the Wye Valley Christian Festival, attracting visitors from throughout Britain. A more pro-active stance on pastoral care was shown by the building on chapel land of six bungalows for the elderly in 1983 and 1988. A new Family Centre has also been built and was officially opened in 2000, providing rooms for children's and youth activities. And today the chapel's message reaches a wider audience than just the village—it can be found on the internet.

Worship: Christ Church, Gorsley

While the rise in the numbers of the Baptist congregation in Victorian times was no doubt due to the evangelising zeal of Pastor Hall, there was also a natural increase in population. Less than a generation after the building of the new Baptist Chapel the Anglican community had also grown sufficiently to require its own minister and Gorsley was recognised as a separate ecclesiastical district in 1872. However, it was to be another twenty years before Christ Church, Gorsley would be built and in the meantime, like its Baptist counterpart, worship was held in a new school. Officially known as Gorsley National School it was opened in 1872 with 36 pupils on the roll.

The new ecclesiastical parish of Gorsley with Clifford's Mesne was formed out of the parishes of Newent (Gloucestershire) and Linton (Herefordshire). In 1882 the Ecclesiastical Commissioners approved St Peter's, Clifford's Mesne as the parish church with Christ Church, Gorsley as a Chapel of Ease or daughter church. Before this villagers in Herefordshire had to walk to St Mary's, Linton for worship while those in Gloucestershire had to walk to St Mary's, Newent and were involved with the church activities there.

The foundation stone for Christ Church was laid in May 1892 and the completed building was dedicated just over a year later in July 1893 by the Bishop of Gloucester. The land for the building had been given by the Onslow Trustees, Mr R. Foley Onslow having previously donated the land for the village school. The cost of the church itself was reported at £1,030 much of which was raised by voluntary dona-

Christ Church, Gorsley

tions, while the incumbent, the Revd S.R. Cambie gave the large sum of £403 11s 9d.

The stone for the building came from Mr Onslow's quarry at a cost of threepence per yard. Designed by Samuel Rollinson and Sons of Chesterfield, the building work was carried out by John Bidmead of Newent. A report of the time describes it well:

> A cruciform edifice of local stone with Bath stone dressing, in
> Early English style, consisting of a chancel, nave, organ
> chamber and West turret containing one bell.

But a later commentator, David Verey in his volume in the *Buildings of England* series, dismissed it as 'of hideous but very well executed stone work'. Local people, with more Christian charity than Mr Verey, love their church, as the list of bequests testifies. In 1896 communion plate, an oak communion table and a brass lectern were given by various parishioners. To commemorate the incumbency (1914-1946) of Revd W.H. Fane-Dickinson, a brass font ewer was presented. A new bell was donated in 1967 and in 1992 the Sharpe Trust loaned the present bell.

When the National School closed in 1926 the building began to be used for church and village activities and in 1954 it was purchased from the diocesan authorities by a trust set up through the Parochial Church

Christ Church, Gorsley, interior

The Mothers Union, Christ Church, in the 1950s

Council. The Church Hall, as it was known, was widely used for many years but the rising cost of repairs forced the trust to sell it in 1992.

The money realised was put into a trust fund which the trustees registered as a 'charity for ecclesiastical and other purposes'. A supplementary document (called 'Standing Orders') directs the trustees as to how the money generated by the fund can be distributed and, in keeping with the original trust deeds of 1954, this is to be for the benefit of the parish.

In 1997 the Upper Room was built at the West end of the church for meetings and the Sunday School. It was opened in November of that year by the then oldest and youngest members of the congregation, Mrs F. Coleman and Master Timothy Oastler. The Bishop of Gloucester, the Rt Revd David Bentley officially dedicated the Upper Room at a special service at Epiphany 1998.

The children who attend the Sunday School make a special study of the many wild flowers and grasses which grow in the churchyard—the number of species attracts interested visitors from spring until autumn, when the grass is cut.

In 1985, in line with many other parishes, Christ Church, Gorsley and St Peter's, Clifford's Mesne, became a United Benefice with St

The former school and church hall

Mary's Newent, sharing the ministry throughout the district. Ten years later the parish joined Newent in a local ecumencial partnership with the Methodist Church and in 1998 the United Benefice extended its local ecumenical partnership to include the Baptists.

And so, today, the religious divisions of two hundred years ago have been brought together. But without these liturgical differences it is likely that the community would not have developed so strongly and certainly there would have been no impetus for education.

Schooldays

It was only with the coming of the 1870 Education Act that any attempt was made to regulate children's education nationally. Schools could range from the excellent to the awful—the fictional Dotheboys Hall in Dickens' *Nicholas Nickleby* was an exaggeration, but only just. Many different types of school had developed, partly because admission to many schools and all universities had been restricted to members of the Church of England. In some areas this could be hard on pupils who came from non-Anglican families, but in Gorsley, with both the Goffs School and the National School, education was available to all.

The problem was whether the children would attend. The head-master of the National School. Mr W. Becket, noted in 1873:

> 28th March: I had to punish three children for attempting to play truant. Each child received two stripes of the cane on each hand. Children attend horses at the plough rather than attend school. There is no co-operation with the parents.
> 10th October: Cider making has commenced - yet another cause of poor attendance. This irregularity embarrasses the work of the whole school ... I shall indeed be thankful when compulsory attendance reaches these remote parts.

But for families dependent on the land, every hand, however small, was needed at times and until 1890 the school was fee-paying, which must also have been a disincentive for parents. The fees were twopence (less than 1p) per week or one shilling and tenpence (9p) per quarter. The school records note that some children paid only one (old) penny per week. Whatever the reason, when the Board of Governors examined the school a few months later, more than half the 88 pupils were absent.

Possibly the poor attendance also had something to do with the headmaster, who was dismissed 'for misconduct' the following year. Twelve months later the school had 100 children in three classes. To accommodate them was one large room (64 ft x 24 ft) a smaller one (32 ft x 18 ft) set at right angles on the south side, which with outbuildings, formed a quadrangle in which the pupils could exercise. These outbuildings included toilets, but we have no record of their type. Perhaps they were better than the ones at Gorsley Goffs School which were 'just a plank of wood with three holes in it and three buckets under each hole. These were emptied once a week by the caretaker'.

The washing facilities at Gorsley Goffs were not much better. Before mains water came to the village the water for the school had to be drawn from a well in the school grounds. The water, a villager remembers, was pumped by hand, usually by a pupil, into a tank in the roof.

> This water supplied three washbasins (cold water only) for hand washing. Before the installation of the basins, the children washed in hand bowls. In winter when it was very cold, the tank in the roof would freeze, so water for the school was

School certificate, National School

fetched from a nearby home ... The school had no central heating, only a tortoise coke stove. It was the pupils' job to keep the coke scuttles filled ... almost a full time job in the cold weather.

Children brought their own food to school for lunch. For a hot drink the pupils would bring a mug with cocoa powder in it to be topped up with hot water which had been boiled on top of the stove. At the National School the long-serving and much-respected headmaster, Mr Martin, began providing cocoa for pupils in November 1903. After an initially difficult start with a succession of temporary headteachers, the school had settled down under Miss Elizabeth Smithers with, as the Governors noted 'an improvement in intelligence and discipline'. By 1890 there were five classes at the National School, the younger ones doing their lessons with slates and chalk, while the older pupils used foolscap paper and pencil. This was also the system at Gorsley Goffs School, and in later years the older children were allowed pen and ink.

Mr Martin arrived at the school in 1892. He must have been a strict disciplinarian—and probably no bad thing—in November of that year one boy was caught stealing other children's dinners. The boy was taken to Newent Police Court where he was convicted of stealing.

In 1903 the school came under the auspices of Gloucester County Council and was known as Newent-Gorsley Council School. There were, at that time, 73 on the register, but over the following years numbers declined and by 1925 only 39 children were at the school and it closed the following year, pupils transferring to Picklenash or Gorsley Goffs.

The school took children until the age of 14, after which they either left or transferred on to higher education. One former pupil recalls those days: 'Most of the girls went into service, some staying locally, others going as far away as Bognor Regis. The boys worked on smallholdings, farms, sawmills or with the forestry workers ... There were no school uniforms, clothes were usually hand-me-downs or outgrown clothes from neighbours' children. Dresses were made from secondhand clothes, unpicked and made to a different size. The boys usually wore jerseys, short trousers and boots'.

The National School in the 1920s

The headmaster, Mr Warren, reported on this in 1920. 'Attendance at the school dropped' he noted, 'when there was a medical inspection ... Causes for absence may be put down to resentment, shame because of poor clothing and vermin-bitten bodies or indifference'.

The prevalence of disease in those pre-inoculation days comes as a surprise to the modern reader. In 1922 Goffs School was closed by the School Medical Officer for two periods of a fortnight in February and March because of influenza. The following year it closed for 12 days due to chickenpox. Outbreaks of measles, influenza and other illnesses caused the school to be closed for weeks at a time, but the most serious epidemic was in November 1934. The headmaster's report states:

> November 1st 1934. An outbreak of diphtheria at the school closes it for two weeks; swabs were taken from the children and many were found to be carriers of the germ. More swabs were taken and children sent to the isolation hospital [in Ross]. The Chief Medical Officer and the County Bacteriologist visited the school. All children and staff were swabbed and the CMO ordered the school closed for two weeks.
> November 16th 1934. The CMO extended the closure of the school until Nov 23rd. Some children were still absent after 18 weeks since the diphtheria epidemic began.

Gorsley Goffs British School

HEAD MASTER: M. W. WARREN
(Associate College Preceptors)

Report for Term ending ...August... 1919

Name Emily Jordan   Junior.

Age 12·6   Average Age in Class 12·6

	POSITION	REMARKS
English	8	Good.
Arithmetic	10	Weak.
History & Geography	14	Very Fair.
Drawing & Nature Study	7	Good
Needlework (12 in class)	1	Very Good.
Handwork		

No. in Class 21   Position in Class 8

Conduct Excellent.

No. of times Absent 9   No. of times late 5

School re-opens Sept 9

(Signed)

                                        Class Teacher

M. W. Warren Head Master

School report, Gorsley Goffs School

It was to be another eight years before immunisation against this deadly disease became routine.

But there were more joyful causes for absence. Days off are recorded for the Coronation (of George VI), for several Royal Weddings, a Royal Visit (to Hereford), visits to the Three Counties Show, the Gloucester Fair and, of course, for daffodil picking. The flowers were picked by the pupils and sent to London hospitals. In 1929 a record 536 bunches were sent.

The war brought unwelcome changes to the school as the arrival of evacuee children meant overcrowding and much disruption (see chapter XII). Despite this, the school weathered the storms and, following post-war legislation, entered the second half of the twentieth century as Gorsley Goffs Endowed Primary School—'a school to remember with its caring family atmosphere and opportunities for learning,' a former pupil recalls. 'The school uniform of grey and maroon was worn with pride'.

In June 1923 the then headmaster, Mr Warren, had noted that 'the new cloakroom is now in use' and the following month the new extension to the school had been formally opened. This at last provided three classrooms in the school 'one for each teacher'. It was to be forty years on before any further improvements were put down

Gorsley Goffs School in the 1930s

in the headmaster's report. In June 1963 work started on flush toilets and by the time the autumn term started that year electricity had been connected. Two further classrooms were added in 1967 although these were semi-permanent structures. The other major event of the 1966/67 school year was an educational excursion to France, Belgium and Holland. 'This is the first time in the history of the school that such a journey has been attempted' wrote the headmaster, Mr Witts.

Stanley Witts is remembered with affection and respect by several generations of pupils. He worked tirelessly to improve the school facilities and broaden the interests and education of the children. He became headmaster in 1955, having served as assistant head for six years and particularly encouraged organised sport—introducing a running track in Pound Lane, for example—and music. The Stanley Witts room in the school (currently used for IT) was originally dedicated as a music room in recognition of his enthusiasm.

Chapter V
Gorsley Village Hall

Towards the end of the Second World War it was decided that a purpose-built village hall was needed in Gorsley, and five weeks after VE Day, on June 15th 1945, a meeting was held at Gorsley Goffs School where the headmaster, Mr Warren, was elected chairman of the hall committee. At the meeting it was decided that:

> A record should be kept of all subscribers, large and small and should be displayed in a permanent and prominent manner, so that future Gorsley people shall know by whose generosity the Hall was made possible.

The fundraising got off to a good start with a gymkhana held at Two Parks Farm by kind permission of Mr Higgins. More than six hundred people attended, raising £225 towards the cost of acquiring land and building the hall. Other events included whist drives, fêtes, cherry feasts, dances (held at Linton Village Hall), skittles competitions at the New Inn (now the Roadmaker) and, of course, a Christmas Draw. Additionally, toys were made for a Toy Fair, clay pigeon shoots were held in one of the fields at Mr Sterry's farm and a bowling competition, first prize a joint of meat, was also popular.

In 1948 Mr Phillips offered a piece of land in Quarry Lane, just under one and a half acres in size. A deposit of £10 was made against the purchase price of £100. The fundraising continued, including the collection and sale of old woollen clothes by Mrs Clough, the Treasurer of the committee, and a 'Pound Night' social where the entrance fee was something which weighed one pound—these items

Gorsley Village Hall today

were then sold at the end of the evening. To mark the Festival of Britain in 1951 a fête was held at the school on June 30th; called a Strawberry Feast the event included stalls and sideshows and a bowling for a pig competition.

By spring 1957 the land for the hall had been purchased and, after much discussion, it was decided that plans for the hall should go ahead, but it was not until July 1963 that work commenced. A year later, on July 18th 1964, the Village Hall, which had taken 19 years to come to fruition and had cost £3694 11s 6d, was officially opened by Mrs Warren, widow of the late chairman of the committee.

Since then it has been used for all manner of village activities: dances and discos, talks and toddler groups and of course, meetings and get-togethers. In 1991 it was decided to build an extension which would allow for better storage for playgroup equipment, provide a room for small social gatherings or committee meetings, improve kitchen and toilet facilities and allow access for wheelchair users. This extension was opened in May 1993.

The hall was the focus for Millennium celebrations on the Fun Day, May 6th 2000 with refreshments on hand for the many visitors who had come to take part and enjoy the sideshows, events and stalls. In the evening Dick Brice entertained a 'full house' with Forest songs and anecdotes and the day ended with a firework display on the land behind the hall, best viewed from the hall car park!

CHAPTER VI
Gorsley Horticultural Society

'What can we do to improve the gardens and allotments in the area?' That was the question debated by a group of Gorsley parish councillors as they made their way back from a meeting in Linton one day in 1925. Someone—it is not recorded who—suggested a flower show, and from the seed of this chance conversation the Horticultural Society for Gorsley and District bloomed. Formed in May 1925 the Society covered Gorsley, Kilcot, Upton Bishop, Kempley and Four Oaks with Oxenhall joining in 1927. The first president was Mr Boxwell of Linton Hall and local headmaster Mr Warren was secretary and treasurer.

The annual flower show, the first of which was held on Wednesday August 5th 1925 at Linton Hall, was not confined to exhibits of flowers, fruit and vegetables. Home produce, including jams and preserves were judged and children's games and sports competitions were part of the event. For those without green fingers there were other events and competitions: children's fancy dress, collection of wildflowers, making a scarecrow, baby show, ladies' ankle competition and climbing the greasy pole. Two skittle alleys, one for men and one for ladies, were set up for bowling for the pig—always a popular event in those difficult days when a pig would keep a family in meat for some time. One of the highlights, at some shows, was the ladies trying to catch the greasy pig—this too was a great prize and always great fun for the spectators!

During the war years no show was held, but in August 1945 a small show, with only 40 classes, was held in Gorsley Goffs School and exhibitors were requested to give their exhibits to be sold for the

Prizewinning veg at the Flower Show

benefit of the Red Cross and the local Welcome Home Fund. From 1946 to 1951 the shows were held at Cherry Farm, including the Silver Jubilee show in 1950, which attracted over 600 entries. In honour of their then President, the Society donated a silver cup, the T.E. Aston Cup, to be presented to the competitor who gained most points in any one show.

The society and the show continued to flourish until the early 1960s. In 1962 over 1,000 peple attended the show (now being held at Pound Farm) with 546 entries for 111 classes.

At this show the children's sports had 13 different classes and there were nine classes for ladies and gents including 'Musical chairs on a bicycle'. There was also a fancy dress parade and a Punch and Judy show, but the highlight of the day was a go-kart demonstration, which was a new feature for the show.

These were the golden years of the Flower Show, as two residents, who were children in the 1960s, recall: 'On the morning of the Show my family would rise extremely early, spending hours trying to clean,

*Children's fancy dress competition. Probably 1953, Coronation year
—note the TV picture!*

pick and arrange the best of the fruit, veg and flowers which covered the whole of the back lawn, but their efforts were usually rewarded at the end of the day with some form of recognition. I entered various children's classes for drawing, painting, miniature gardens, collection of wild flowers, pressed flowers, collection of cabbage white butterflies and the feeling of competition was great. An enjoyable day which ended late evening with a drink at the local pub'.

It was also good fun for a young lad: 'The most memorable annual event was the Gorsley Flower Show ... I used to enter classes for: the nosegay of wildflowers (large bunch in a 2lb jam jar); the posy of wildflowers (small bunch, neatly arranged with a doiley in a 1lb jam jar); miniature garden (in a seed box); collection of vegetables—for which my dad made me a display stand; and the Victoria sponge. There would be a wide range of sideshows. I used to help by sticking up on the skittles. The prize was often a pig, hence competition was serious. Many times after everything else had been cleared away the men would still be bowling even up till they needed to use torches to see. I later ran the rifle range using my own airgun'.

In 1965 the date of the show, which had always been the Wednesday after the August Bank Holiday, changed to the last Saturday in July, due to the August Bank Holiday shifting to the end of the month. The last full Flower Show was held in 1970, but this and the Bulb Show held the following spring, made a loss. It was decided to suspend the activities of the Society 'owing to the lack of support and the Society's inability to elect officers'.

But by 1977 there was a renewed interest in horticulture in the village and a Gardening Club was formed. The old competitive spirit has dimmed, but the club continues with winter meetings in the Village Hall and summer meetings spent visiting open gardens and occasionally a garden centre.

Chapter VII
Pound Farm

Among the many farms and smallholdings which are part of Gorsley and Kilcot, Pound Farm is unique. It is run by a charity—Salter's Hill Charity—which was formed in 1984 by three people who had experience of the problems facing young adults with learning difficulties. Two of the founders had been teachers in special schools, the third was a parent of a child with learning difficulties.

Their aim was to create a home where a dozen or so people with learning difficulties could live as normal and independent a family life as possible. They wanted to find a house with a few acres of land so that the home would benefit from producing its own fruit and vegetables. In 1986 Pound Farm came on the market and within two years planning permission had been obtained, alterations and repairs made and the first residents moved in.

Although the charity had raised £150,000 to provide and equip the buildings, fundraising did not stop there—it is an ongoing activity organised by the Pound Farm Voluntary Support group, the Friends of Salter's Hill, parents of residents, local people, various sponsors and many donations.

In 1993 the charity purchased a house in Gorsley, about a mile from Pound Farm. The house name 'Regina' was changed to 'Ryelands' in a fit of prescience, for a little later a small flock of Ryeland sheep were grazing there. Four young people moved in and in 1999 a studio flat was converted to house two of the residents. A third home, Keepers Cottage at Ledbury, is home to six people.

In each home the residents all have a job to do according to his or her interests and abilities. With workshops, greenhouses, polytun-

Pound Farm

nels, sheep, cows, ducks and chickens all needing attention, outdoor jobs are numerous and varied. At the homes one will also find the Ryeland sheep which are bred for their even temperament. When lambing time comes the residents take charge, even getting up in the middle of the night to make sure everything is alright. The sheep have won several prizes at country shows. Hawthorn the cow also receives her share of attention, especially at milking time.

Indoors of course there is always housework and cooking while the games and hobby rooms are widely used, together with local recreation facilities. Many of the residents are active in local work, helping at playgroups in local schools, garden centres, cafés, farms and local churches, as well as attending courses at colleges. These young people have become very much part of the village community and the homes, which are manned 24 hours a day, have also provided employment for several local people.

Chapter VIII
People and Places

Collecting material for this book has uncovered a miscellany of reminiscences about people who used to live in the area and places that were important at some time in the history of the community. Some of the people were well-known nationally or regionally, others were local 'characters' mentioned by several interviewees. The places trace the growth, movement and decline of local trade over the past hundred years or so. It is an eclectic selection and not in any way definitive.

RUTLAND BOUGHTON - Composer
Born in Aylesbury in 1878, Rutland Boughton was a composer, chiefly of opera and choral works. He founded the original Glastonbury Festival (1914-25) and in 1936 bought Beavan's Hill House, Kilcot, a smallholding with nine acres of land, allegedly saying that as the financial returns from music were so meagre in those days the little farm helped support his large family. He also occasionally hosted outdoor concerts there.

The music of Boughton has been likened to that of Vaughan Williams, but he was also influenced by Wagner. His two best known works are the choral drama *Bethlehem* and his opera *The Immortal Hour*, which enjoyed great contemporary success with over 200 performances. The *Malvern Gazette* records that after some of his concerts he would not wait for the supper that was provided, but went straight back to Kilcot saying he wanted to look after his goats.

Boughton was strongly influenced by socialist and communist ideas and mixed with other artists, writers and musicians with similar views. He was visited at Beavan's Hill by many of these figures

Rutland Boughton and his family at Beavan's Hill House

including George Bernard Shaw and Paul Robeson. Edward Elgar was also a visitor. His political ideas and unconventional private life were not always popular with the establishment and this is thought to be one of the reasons for the eventual demise of the Glastonbury Festival, which failed to find financial backing. He lived at Beavan's Hill House until his death in 1960.

KEVIN ELLIS - Inventor

A respected and well-loved character was Kevin Ellis, who, with his sister May, lived in Kilcot all his life. Born in 1903, he had been a prosperous, hardworking young garage proprietor when, at the age of 29, he was suddenly crippled with arthritis. This affected his whole body leaving him with limited mobility. Kevin was virtually locked in a seated position with minimal movement in his neck, shoulders and fingers yet he led an almost independent life. For Mr Ellis was an inventor and designer of great skill and spent many of his waking hours designing gadgets to make himself even more independent.

In his day wheelchairs had not been designed for people with such limited movement so he set about designing a chair for his own special requirements. The chair had to be capable of being operated by himself, even though his elbows were locked with his forearm and upper arm more or less at right angles to each other; he had some finger movement and a little head mobility.

The first chair, not unlike the 'moonbuggy' of later years was made from parts from the Air Ministry Surplus Store, with wheelbarrow wheels, pieces of plywood, lengths of angle iron, nuts, bolts and screws either purchased or donated by friends and neighbours who also undertook the actual manufacture of the chair under Kevin's direction. Two 12-volt batteries powered small electric motors which drove the wheels and allowed for steering by remote control with small movements of elbows and fingers. The chair, which could be used indoors and out, was the first of several, each one an improvement on its predecessor.

Other gadgets which he designed to make life easier included a hook made from a bicycle spoke—a simple idea but a great help in order to reach switches and scratch itches! Other inventions helped

Kevin Ellis in the 'moonbuggy' wheelchair he designed

him to put on his spectacles, answer the telephone, open and close doors and lift him from the chair on to his bed and back again. His chair was even fitted with its own plumbing and also had a tilt mechanism which allowed Kevin to transfer his weight on to his back, to alleviate pressure points.

Kevin and his sister lived on the Aston Ingham road, just up from Kilcot Cross, originally in the house called 'Glendalough', but they later moved a few yards up the road into a purpose-built bungalow named 'Oaklea' after the big oak tree which grew in front of it. The property had a big garden and in the early 1960s Andrew McIntosh recalls 'I was privileged, along with other engineers in the village, including Freddy Underwood and my father, John McIntosh, to be able to help build an even more elaborate machine which could even dig Kevin's garden'.

When not designing gadgets and improvements to his wheel-chairs Kevin Ellis had a part-time job trimming pictures and mounting them on Christmas cards. For this a special guillotine had to be designed so that by a slight nod of the head an electrical impulse would operate the blade.

His disability never stopped him from going out and about in a specially adapted van which held his chair safely in position and he also went on holiday in a caravan adapted to his needs. Although badly crippled he managed to sketch and write his ideas for others to interpret. His cheerful demeanour and determination to be independent guaranteed him a place in the admiration and affection of his neighbours, who were ever ready to help him.

He died in 1975 at the age of 72 and was buried at Christ Church, Gorsley.

A.D. EVANS - Golfer and farmer

Albert David Evans was an outstanding amateur golfer, a well-known breeder of Hereford cattle and a farmer whose methods were often well ahead of their time.

Born at Brecon in 1911 to a farming family, his interest in golf was aroused at school by his science master, Geoffrey Isitt. Despite having lost a finger as a young child, Albert Evans showed an early aptitude for the game and a nine hole course was laid out at the family farm by the former Open Champion, James Braid. In 1932 he played for Wales in the Home International for the first time. He was to

A.D. Evans

continue representing the land of his fathers until 1961, when he captained the Welsh side which beat England for the first time.

During the war years and those immediately following his golfing activities were limited. Among his achievements he was Welsh Champion in 1949 and again in 1961 (at the age of 49, a record that was to stand for 40 years), and semi-finalist in the British Amateur Championship in 1951. He was chairman of the Welsh Golf Union 1972-78 and President 1979-83. For many years he was also a selector for the British Walker Cup side and, as the *Daily Telegraph* said, known in the golfing world as 'a pillar of integrity and kindness'.

In recognition of the part golf played in his life he named his herd of Herefords 'The Bogey Herd'. Albert Evans and his wife, May, had moved to Gloucestershire in the 1930s and he set about building up a prize-winning herd of cattle as well as breeding sheep. He was always keen to embrace new ideas, being one of the first people in the country to purchase a Ferguson tractor which used hydraulics to operate attachments. He also experimented with new strains of grass and clovers. His farming success and personal qualities led to him being in great demand as a judge.

Albert Evans' most lasting contribution to the local community, however, has been the establishment of the Ross-on-Wye Golf Club.

He led a small band of members who bought the site in 1961 and developed it into a noted 18-hole course which opened in 1964. Thanks to Mr Evans' loan of farm machinery and hard work by other members the total cost, including clubhouse, was only £45,000.

Whilst most of his life was spent 'across the border', Albert Evans was rightly proud of his Welsh heritage and his home in Kilcot was renamed 'Newton House' after the family farm. He died in 2000, aged 89.

BEN JAMES - Farmer

Ben James was renowned for the strength of the cider he brewed at Ford Farm in the 1950s. He sold it to pubs in Ross and regularly loaded up his horse and cart to deliver the barrels round the town. Having had a few samples at each inn it was not unknown for a landlord to lift Ben onto the cart, tie the reins in position and tell the horse to go home. With Ben singing lustily in the back, the obedient horse, named Sparking Plug, would take his owner home, through Phocle Green, Upton Bishop, Gorsley and back to Kilcot. Ben also developed a *tendre* for his next-door neighbour, Miss May Ellis, and was inclined to serenade her of an evening when he had been checking his latest brew. She did *not* reciprocate his feelings.

FRED JOHNSON - Woodman

Much of the clearance work at the new Ross-on-Wye Golf Club was carried out by Fred Johnson. Even though he was in his eighties he would walk nearly three miles from his home in Gorsley to the new club site and clear the undergrowth with an axe weighing about 4 lbs. Weather permitting he would work about five hours a day and then walk the three miles home. For a meal he would 'toast a bit of bacon' over one of the fires of the cleared brush that was burning. He always said that it was his active, outdoor life which kept him so fit.

DENNIS POTTER - Writer

The author and playwright, Dennis Potter, is always associated with the Forest of Dean, where he was brought up in a mining family. Many of his best-known TV plays are set in that area, most notably *Pennies from Heaven* and *Blue Remembered Hills*. However, for a short time he lived in Kilcot in the house that is now 'Courtlands'. The property, which was then a small cottage, was extended by the Potters, who later moved to Ross.

The Roadmaker Inn—then

PLACES
THE ROADMAKER INN
The Roadmaker was built in 1847 and was named Roadway Place after its original owner, Mr Benjamin James, who was a roadmaker. The name changed to the New Inn in 1871 and in 1977, after considerable improvement and alterations it was renamed the Roadmaker.

The Moody Cow pub at Upton Bishop was originally called the Duke of Wellington.

GORSLEY SHOPS
When the telephone came to Gorsley the exchange was installed in a room in the Post Office (now The Old Post Office). This remained the village Post Ofice until 1962 when it moved to the village shop (owned by Mr & Mrs Allport) located at the Sugar Tump. When the owners retired in 1969 the Post Office transferred to the Royal Stores on the main road, where it remains to this day.

The Roadmaker Inn—now

The Royal Stores were built in the nineteenth century by Royal Cracknell, hence its name. The face of the stores has changed over the years, the most recent being in 1987 when the front was renewed. Before the Second World War the Stores sold all manner of household items: pails, buckets, coal scuttles and hods, brooms and mops—all were hung up outside along the front of the shop.

Over the years there have been a number of bakers in the village. At Christmas time if the goose or cockerel would not fit into the householder's oven, then it would be taken to the baker for cooking in his large bake oven. One man is remembered for not charging for this which he said was his 'Christmas present' to the families.

The present owners of the Gorsley PO and Stores: Gordon and Diane

LINTON HALL

Built in 1888, it was first known as Quarry House and although it was thought to have been a public house at one time, it was in fact built for the quarry master of Green's Quarry.

PROSPECT ROW

The houses were built in 1840. Six were built with all the families sharing one laundry room!

BEAVAN'S HILL

According to the reminiscences of Mrs May Fishpool (recorded in 1973 when she was 77): 'Beavan's Hill got its name from an old lady who used to wear a crinoline—my dad used to tell me this when he was a boy ... and this old woman had got a great big bonnet on and wide skirts and my father said he used to be so frightened of her and her name was Mary Beavan. And they called the hill Beavan's Hill and Mr Peacock the schoolmaster as lived where Rutland Boughton lived couldn't believe me, but he had to in the end. She was often called Molly which is a nickname for Mary.

'The house where Rutland Boughton lived—it used to be an old public house—The little old-fashioned bungalow opposite used to be a blacksmith's forge'.

KILCOT SHOPS

Before the Second World War there were two shops in Shotts Lane which sold sweets and various necessities; one was run by Mrs Lewis and the other by Mr & Mrs Groves. On Kilcot Hill there was another shop on what is now 'Sunnybank', run by Mr & Mrs Buckland, but

Kilcot Cross

Kilcot Garage, intact and ablaze

this closed during the war. A blind lady, Miss Wood, had a sweet shop on the Aston Ingham road and also on that road, at Blaisdon Cottage opposite the chapel, was a shoe-mender, Mr Underwood. It was cheaper to get him to mend your shoes than the cobbler in Aston Ingham. In 1936 the Kilcot Garage caught fire. It was a wooden structure and was completely destroyed. It was rebuilt in brick in 1938.

Kilcot Post Office has been at various sites around Kilcot Cross. Early in the twentieth century it was run by Mrs Herbert from 'Poona', then Mrs Yeates ran it from 'Westbrook' (then called 'Dak Bungalow'. It then moved to 'Rossmore' and was run by a number of people including Miss Cutter, Gerry O'Keefe and Idris Lane until moving again, just to 'Crossways' (next to 'Rossmore' and now called 'The Old Post Office' and finally back across the road to 'Normanhurst', where it finally closed in the early 1990s.

CHAPTER IX
In Living Memory: Schooldays

This, the most important part of our history, recalls Gorsley and Kilcot in the words of those who have lived and are still living here. Although divided into sections on school, family and work life isn't like that, so some memories span across these artificial divides.

Mary Smith and her brother, Eric Hayward, lived at the Kilcot Inn: 'My brother Eric and I both went to Picklenash School in Newent in the 1920s. I had to walk there—it was about one and a half miles—from the age of five. One of Eric's classmates, Dick Allen, walked even further, from Aston Ingham as he lived just on the Gloucestershire side of the stream that marked the border between Herefordshire and Gloucestershire. But another friend, Walter Warren, who lived on the opposite side of the stream, went to Aston Ingham School.

'There were no school meals, we took sandwiches and the caretaker made cocoa which cost one [old] penny a cup. Eric went on to the [Newent] Grammar School where there was a canteen run by the caretaker, Tom Tilling'.

Frank Huggins, who lived in Gorsley, attended Gorsley Goffs School until 1943 when he was 14. His elder sister, Ruby (now Mrs Ruby Goulding) was a teacher at the school: 'I used to walk to school along the road, which was very quiet—just the occcasional bus—or I'd come back across the fields, scrumping apples or pears from the trees in the summer. I'd take sandwiches for lunch and you could buy milk to drink—a ha'penny for one third of a pint—plus biscuits were sold at six for a penny and Horlicks tablets. I was never very keen on school, but on Friday afternoons if the headmaster Mr

Gorsley Goffs School in the 1930s

Warren was in a good mood we could play football. [Frank went on to play football for Gorsley in the Ross League.]

'If we misbehaved we were sent to stand in the corner, or we'd get hit with a ruler or a stick for more severe offences. I hated Shakespeare and one time during the lesson I was eating an apple hidden under the desk. Mr Warren saw it and hit me on both sides of the head, then told Ruby, who was teaching next door "I've just given your brother the works of Shakespeare!"'

Another lad who was not enamoured of school was Gerald Yeates, of Westbrook, Kilcot: 'I went to Picklenash School from 1935 to 1944 —didn't learn a lot. Before the war I took the Red & White bus there and back at the cost of a penny each way, later there was only a bus to school and you had to walk back. At first I took sandwiches for lunch, but later, during the war, there was a school canteen. The headmaster was a Mr Hudson and discipline was very good'.

Peter Atkinson, who now lives at Kilcot Nurseries, spent his early schooldays at Botloes Green, and went to Picklenash and then Newent Grammar School by bicycle or on foot. He remembers the school meals with pleasure: 'I used to have the school lunches which were cooked on the premises, they cost half a crown [12.5p] a week

The Church of England School in the 1920s

and were very good. All the books, pens and pencils were provided. My grandmother had been to Christ Church School, Gorsley and had used slate and pencils'.

When did the slate and pencils disappear? One former pupil is convinced that they were still in use after the Second World War: 'It must have been in about 1956 that they introduced new technology into the school [Gorsley Goffs]. Pencils and paper replaced our slates and chalks. The hexagonal ones used to roll down the desk, so at one time we were given blue triangular ones'.

Other aspects of school life were also rooted in the early part of the twentieth century: 'In winter the schoolrooms were heated by big circular coke stoves which glowed a deep red when they got going. When it was snowy or wet the fireguard was surrounded by shoes and boots and covered in socks ... With no mains water or drainage, the toilets were of the "bucket and chuck it" variety'.

But for all that, it was a happy place, remembered with affection: 'The headmaster for all my time there was the legendary Stan Witts. He took a real personal interest in every pupil at the school. He could be very strict when he needed to but kindness itself at most times. As well as giving us a good academic launch we were always encouraged to take part in the various musical and drama events that were held. This was recognised a few years ago when the new music room was dedicated to Stan. There was also lots of sport. As well as cricket and football Stan taught us "hurly-burly", basically touch rugby. In the summer we took part in athletics.

'The school was so good that a coach was run from Ross to bring children to it and when many village schools closed it was Gorsley that survived. It had three classes with two years in each class. We got a good start with Mrs Clough, the infant teacher. A wonderfully warm person she enthused us all. She kept a jar of sweets on top of the piano for special rewards, but would also make use of the slipper when necessary. Right from the start in her class there was the principle of giving children responsibility; there were monitors for everything. When we were in the second year she even got those of us who were good at reading to help the younger ones.

'Life at Gorsley School was good, my only negative memory related to school meals. They were cooked in Ross then delivered to the school in insulated containers. I remember everything being overcooked with watery vegetables amd leathery meat. Packed lunches were far preferable'.

Gorsley Goffs School Athletic Team

Playtime

'All work and no play makes Jack a dull boy' as the saying goes, and for children growing up in Gorsley and Kilcot, there was plenty of opportunity for play. As well as team games, such as cricket, football and rounders, children enjoyed traditional games such as conkers and marbles. Girls would play hopscotch, skipping, hoop and stick and whip and top. Many pastimes were country pursuits, and many memories remain:

'We used to play on Kilcot common, girls and boys together. There were two pools there and we caught scarlet newts in them. There was a football pitch on the common and gypsies used to camp there too'. (Mary Smith)

'I used to play fox and hounds in the woods all around here, with one person acting as the fox and the rest chasing after as hounds. At Hillhouse Grove in Gorsley there used to be a wood which went all the way to Oxenhall and Brockmoor Head. And I would follow the real hounds on foot too. I knew an old countryman, Harry Taylor from Beavan's Hill. He was known as "Whippet" and I used to go over to Payford Bridge and Redmarley with him, otter hunting in the River Leadon. I never saw him catch one, though. We used to go swimming too, in the pond at Briery Hill—I

Gypsies on Kilcot common

Fishing at Briery Hill

learnt to swim in the brook and in winter we would go skating on the pond opposite the shop on Kilcot Hill'. (Eric Hayward)

Frank Huggins remembers the school breaks too: 'We would play fox and hounds in the lunch hour at school and were often late back for our lessons. As well as football we played hockey too, using home-made sticks. I had a tooth knocked out by the ball'.

'During the war we weren't allowed to play ball games at school in case we broke a window. I never played football or cricket, but enjoyed darts and skittles'. (Gerald Yeates)

After the war things were easier: 'Summer holidays seemed to last for weeks and the evenings stay light until quite late. I can remember Mr Howard, from Gloucester, coming round in his ice cream van. He was always happy, kind and gentle and his ice creams were delicious. Sometimes I went to market in the holidays and was fascinated to hear the auctioneer for the first time. Other highlights of the holiday would be a trip to town, picnics on the Malvern Hills and visits to the seaside'.

But life was still centred on the home: 'We were a close family and I played games with cousins and friends, such as cricket, tennis, hopscotch, hide and seek and marbles. Many of these were played in

The school play 'Oliver Twist' in 1931

the road or the Sugar Tump [Gorsley] as there was less traffic in those days. In the evenings aunts and uncles would call for a game of cards, ludo or similar as we didn't have televisions or computers. In fact electricity was not available until the early sixties'. (Dora Powell, née Fishpool)

The introduction of electricity was to bring new pastimes, as the following memoir of the 1960s illustrates: 'Our social life was largely self made. We climbed trees, played football in the fields and cricket in the road with a Sandoe's fruit box as a wicket. A very popular pastime was to build 'dillies', made from a plank of wood with a Sandoe's box fixed to the back as a seat and old pram wheels, the rear ones large and the front ones smaller but on a movable axis to provide steering with a rope tied to the two ends. My cousin, Henry Davis, went one better, fitting a steeringwheel attached to levers and strings underneath. Our favourite route was the hill by Oliver Taylor's; with practice we could start further and further up the hill, reach the corner faster and get round it without running through Mr Hooper's hedge. We then had to avoid the brook at the bottom. We were not very happy when the four bungalows were built on one of our favourite sledding hills on Quarry Lane.

'When we were in our early teens Mr Carter, a retired police sergeant, started a youth club at the church hall. We played badminton, darts and table football, ate crisps and chocolate and drank coke. Brian Pritchard and I used a reel-to-reel tape recorder to record his record collection and "Top of the Pops" to give us some music'. (Tony Davis)

CHAPTER X
In Living Memory: Family Life and Leisure

If we look back one hundred years to see how families lived then, one of the main differences is that, unlike today, most families stayed within the village or immediate surrounding area. Marriages were often between neighbouring families and thus many people were surrounded by cousins, uncles and aunts as well as the immediate family.

Mary Davies (née Phillips), born at the beginning of the twentieth century, grew up in one such close-knit family. 'My parents started married life at Standfast, Kilcot Hill. My grandfather Phillips lived at the other end of the village and each year lent one of his fields to the Gospel Tent meeting. My other Gramp (Overton) farmed at Babylon, Beavan's Hill'.

A family group, Lower House, 1898

As this letter shows a pig was a valuable commodity,
as good as money to settle debts

Families worked hard, each member having to take a share in the daily chores. As far as possible people tried to be self-sufficient, growing their own fruit and vegetables in the garden or small-holding, keeping hens for eggs and eating and—if they could—keeping a pig or two.

Pigs were kept in a sty in one corner of the garden. Eric Hayward remembers that when it was time for the pig to be killed the slaugh-terman, Mr Walter Davies, known as 'Piggy' or 'Pig-sticker' Davies used to come on his bicycle. The carcase would be hung for a few days then cut in half lengthways, with the entrails falling into a strate-gically placed bath. 'Our mother made faggots and also brawn from the head which she boiled up with a fowl. We also ate chitterlings (pig's innards) well cleaned and turned every day for several days and then boiled. We made our own lard and pork scratchings and used the pig's bladder as a football. As the saying goes "nothing was wasted except the pig's squeal'".

Often one half of the pig would be given to a neighbour or friend until it was time for his pig to be slaughtered, then he would give his half of his pig on to a friend or neighbour—eventually it all evened up with no-one losing out—a good system before widespread use of fridges and freezers because the meat was used up before it could deteriorate. As well as pigs and boiling fowl, the main source of meat was rabbit. 'We had rabbit three or four times a week, there was always a rabbit stock pot on the range' recalls Gerald Yeates. The family also kept chickens and ducks.

Frank Huggins remembers Walter Davies or sometimes Bill Selwyn coming round to kill the pig. 'The pig was then hung up above the dairy and cured with long bars of salt. We ate plain home-cooked food, but there was plenty of it. As well as our own pig meat there was lots of rabbit, plenty of vegetables and fruit in the season. And we had plenty of milk, cream, eggs and cider. There were two casks of cider, one for the family and one rough for the "scroungers" who never helped out at harvest time or anything'.

Frank helped on the farm with the milking and haymaking when he was a boy, standing on the ricks to stamp down the hay. 'I had to be careful not to go too near the edges. Casks of cider were hung round the horses necks, but as haymaking couldn't stop, tots of cider stored in cows' horns helped your thirst—later on we used jam jars instead'.

He also got a Saturday job at Cook's bakery in Newent (in 1940 a full day's work, from 7.30 am, earned half a crown, [12.5p]) and remembers bread being delivered on a cart, covered by a tarpaulin—boys would sometimes hide underneath to pinch the bread. Bread was also baked by Ernie Fishpool in Gorsley in a cordwood oven which gave it a special, delicious flavour.

Eric Hayward remembers bread being delivered in a van and getting fish from Mr Usher who came round with a horse and cart. But for most families the garden, smallholding or farm was the main source of food, with other necessities either coming from the few small local shops or delivered by C&F Thurston of Newent who provided groceries, paraffin and pig meal in a van. Orders placed on Tuesdays would be delivered on Fridays.

Gerald Yeates, and many others, recall the shops—especially the sweet shops—they knew as children in the 1930s and 1940s. 'There were two sweet shops, that also sold necessities, in Shotts Lane, one run by Mrs Lewis and one by Mr & Mrs Groves. Peter James' (of Tan Lan, Kilcot) father had a little shop charging up batteries. Mr & Mrs Buckland ran a shop on Kilcot Hill in what is now "Sunnybank"; it closed during the war. There was a shop along the Aston Ingham road run by a blind lady, Miss Wood; barley sugar cost a farthing. A trader used to bring round jars of sweets—you could get a free clock with six jars of boiled sweets!'.

Mary Smith remembers Mrs Buckland's shop, too, where 'You could buy sherbert and sweets for a halfpenny. When the buses started to operate, *The Citizen* newspaper was deposited at Kilcot Cross where there used to be a triangle of grass in the middle of the road, and the Maddocks boys, Jo and Dennis, used to deliver them'.

Mary was born at the Kilcot Inn, which her parents ran from 1922 and which she and her husband later ran until his death in 1987. Her parents had a smallholding with animals at the pub, and the inn had its own cider mill and press. 'We used a horse to operate it, going round and round. There were hair sheets on top, rather like coir

The Kilcot Inn, in the 1930s
with Mary and Eric Hayward and Dorothy Sysum

matting to crush and filter the apple pulp. My brother Eric [Hayward] and I helped collect apples and pears and helped with the haymaking too'.

Eric remembers that the Kilcot Inn used to be a meeting place for the local farmers who did deals there—often out of hours—and also for the local pigeon club. 'The pub regulars used to arrive by foot, bicycle or horse and cart. There was no breathalyser in those days. The pub sold a cider called "Stunum" which it did!—they'd be immobile after only a pint. Some people walked all the way from Newent to sample it and people came from Aston Ingham to the Kilcot Inn'. Eric doesn't mention how people walked back after drinking the cider!

The Roadmaker pub in Gorsley was called the New Inn in those pre-war days and after playing football in the field opposite, Eric and the rest of the team would have a bath in the garage of the pub. This was an improvement from washing the mud off in the brook.

Until mains water came to the community (1956) people either had their own well or fetched it from a nearby spring. The spring on Kilcot Common was used by several families on the hill.

Peter Atkinson, of Kilcot Nurseries remembers visiting the original cottage which stood on the site of his present home when it was occupied by his great-aunt Claire. It was a one-up, one-down with an

Gorsley AFC, winners of the Ross League in 1949

outside toilet—a 'two-holer', the smaller one for the children—and water came from a well. 'The coming of mains water was wonderful. Before that all the water for "Hillcrest" and for cider-making had to be brought across the road. The original cottage had to use well water and all the irrigation for the crops was provided by using a Lister piston engine and a ram pump to lift water from the well'.

Mary Smith adds: 'Before mains water we pumped water up from the well and carried it in buckets. Clothes were washed in a boiler with water heated with a fire of sticks and coal under—the same boiler was used to steam the Christmas pudding'.

Mains gas was laid along the Newent and Aston Ingham to Kilcot roads in 1955/56, several years before electricity came to the area. The Kilcot Inn had gas lights with mantles, before that they had oil lamps; trimming the wicks and topping up with paraffin was quite a job. Most families had oil lamps and candles for lighting.

Frank Huggins' family had a Villiers two-stroke generator which powered the lights. 'Later this was replaced by a Lister engine. My father had milked the cows using a Moon Box for lighting—this was a sort of paraffin lantern and was liable to go out'.

With no TV in those pre-war days, families had to make their own entertainment. Some families, like the Haywards, had a 'cat's whisker' radio. When accumulator battery radios came along the accumulators were taken to Charlie Watkins in Gorsley or Percy James at Kilcot to be topped up.

Mary Smith remembers that amateur dramatics were organised by Eileen Cook of Alway House and there were plays in Newent. The flower shows and fêtes of Gorsley and Aston Ingham were a major attraction and she remembers dancing on the lawn of the Aston Ingham rectory one evening after the fête.

Otherwise social life centred round the church or chapel. Eric Hayward went to Sunday School at Aston Ingham in the morning, at Christ Church in the afternoon and then sang in the choir at Aston Ingham in the evening. He had to walk between the two and passed the time kicking a football along—until the Christ Church vicar confiscated it!

In the 1950s and early 1960s Dora Powell (née Fishpool) recalls: 'Sundays were special, but different, a quiet day of rest, the opportunity to attend Chapel and Sunday School. The older members of my family often slept in the afternoon, which I couldn't understand

*The skittles team (top) was thriving in those pre-TV days,
as was the darts team (below)*

then, but I can appreciate now. Bath time was in the evening then off to bed with stories read by candlelight'.

Electricity was not to reach the community until 1963, a year after the motorway was built. Until the end of the 'Swinging Sixties' life in the community would have been recognisable to any visitor from before the war.

Dora Powell remembers the rural life: 'Having a smallholding meant that our garden was always full of flowers, trees, fruit and vegetables. The daffodils on the bank were like a golden carpet and I used to help to pick and bunch them ready for market. If I disappeared for any length of time I could often be found in the raspberry canes, probably eating more than I was putting in the punnet.

'We kept small animals and it was great to watch the chicks hatch out. We nurtured them in the house in a box on the Rayburn until they were strong enough to go outside ... I can remember the day my grandmother was shocked and upset because the hens had been savaged by a dog or a fox. The pigs lived in the barn and Gran would often spend the night with them when the sow was farrowing to ensure that everything was well. I enjoyed mixing their food and watching them grow. After about twelve months they would be sold, apart from one or two which would be kept for bacon.

'We often went on long walks round the village and in the woods to pick and learn about wild flowers. We also looked for birds' nests and tried to identify the birds from their eggs. Collecting ripe blackberries from the hedgerows was another pastime and Mr Brown from Ross would come out to buy them'.

But for Andrew McIntosh the move from Little Gorsley to Kilcot was a traumatic event. 'This was back in June 1954. Gone were the days of quiet country lanes on which travelled the occasional pony and trap, this was modern living. We had moved from a cottage in a quiet back lane to (as far as I was concerned) a main arterial road. It was in fact the B4222 road from Kilcot Cross to the A40 at The Lea via Aston Ingham. I actually saw two cars pass that day, apart from the removal van which carried all our worldly goods to our new home'.

And some things never change. The flooding of Ell Brook for example. Andrew McIntosh tells this tale: 'After Ford Farm the road descends quite sharply to the brook, which runs under the road. During the winter, when it rained or the snow melted, the brook used to flood which caused the road to be flooded to a depth of a few feet. My brother and some of his friends and myself used to defy our parents and ride through the flood. Why was it me who always hit the pothole or brick under the murky water ending up the focus of humorous attention as I dragged myself and my bike back home to face Mum's wrath and then being banned for hanging around with the older boys "who would only lead me into mischief".

An American colleague of narrator Tony Davis found the following description of life in Gorsley in the 1950s and early 1960s hard to believe:

'Until Dad became a postman, we derived our entire living from this smallholding [Chancery Cottage]. The land comprised some six acres and its use was fairly mixed and intensive. We also bought some fields for grazing and hay in Sargent's Lane. I was given my first bike to enable me to ride over and bring the cattle back for milking.

'The home land was made up of a large orchard growing cherries, plums, pears and apples (Bramley cookers and eaters). All these were picked and taken to market in Gloucester. My cousin Alfie Johnson used to provide the transport with his Ford 100E and later Morris van. From a young age my job was to scare the birds off the cherries. Each group of trees had an old sheet of galvanised iron hanging up with an assortment of scrap iron attached to a string leading up to the house. Every now and then I would pull the string and frighten off the starlings and pigeons. As I got older Dad got me an air rifle and then a shotgun to help with this.

'Also in the orchard we had cider apples and pears. These had to be really ripe, so were picked off the ground and bagged up. Shaking the trees to get them down was a bit risky, but picking them up could also be a tricky job if the cattle had been in the orchard recently!

'When I was very young there was a cider mill in what is now Mill Cottage, behind the house of Miss Baldwin. We used to put our fruit in with that of the Aubreys and Miss Baldwin. The apples would be put into a large circular trough and Artie Clifford's horse would push round the mill wheel crushing them to pulp. Then the juice was squeezed out of the pulp in a press. This was transferred to barrels for maturing. We always had a 40 gallon barrel at home and Dad used to say I learned to walk by toddling out to the shed with my cup! In later years we sent the apples and pears to either Bulmers in Hereford or Westons in Much Marcle. We also had an area for soft fruit—strawberries, raspberries, black and redcurrants and goose-berries. These also went to market together with Esther Reed's and daffodils from the garden.

'We always had a milk cow and chickens for eggs (and occasion-ally lunch). In addition at different times we kept pigs, beef cattle and sheep for wool. I quite often helped feed and water the stock before going to school. During wet weather this entailed a hard trudge through deep mud. When it was frosty it could be even more difficult as there was no mains water and it had to be pulled out of an underground tank a bucketful at a time. Often the lid would be frozen down and then I had to break the ice with stones before throwing in my bucket on the end of a piece of string.

'Before mains water came to the village some houses had their own well, as we did, others used a communal one near where the stream runs at the bottom of Warren's Pitch. Our well was originally fitted with a bucket but then we became really sophisticated when Dad installed a pipe with a pump in the kitchen. We also had a large tank beside the kitchen wall into which the rainwater was collected off the roof. Hence we had well water for drinking and cooking and rain water for washing.

'When mains water was installed Dad built a bathroom. Previously we had all washed at the kitchen sink and had a bath in a galvanised iron bath in front of the kitchen fire on a Friday night. The toilet was outside, the output of which Dad dug into his vegetable patch—and very effective it was too.

'Heating and cooking was provided by a coal/wood-fired range in the kitchen, later to be supplemented by a bottled gas oven. The frost would make some pretty pictures on the bedroom windows of a winter's morning. Lighting was by paraffin lamps and candles.

'In the mid-1950s Dad bought a Lister diesel-powered generator. This gave us 110 volt DC power. Norman Gooch did the wiring. We only had one power socket. That was in the kitchen, so Mum could use an electric iron instead of putting flat irons on the fire. What a contrast to today when we need at least four sockets in every room, plus connections for TV aerials, phone and internet. Some of the other people who installed generators also bought TVs. My aunt, Florrie Johnson, was one. I used to go down there on a Friday evening to sit with her, her children and grandchildren to watch it— a very full sitting room!'.

CHAPTER XI
In Living Memory: Working Life

The most recent census return for Gorsley (1991) shows that of those people who were in employment almost all worked outside the village. But at the beginning of the twentieth century almost everyone worked within walking distance of their home on their own or neighbouring land. Frank Huggins recalls the working life of his father and grandfathers:

Working life at the turn of the century: Tree-felling

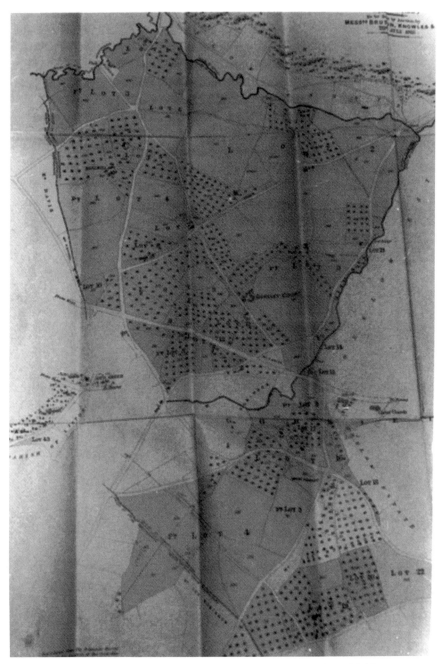

Map of the Onslow Estate properties auctioned in 1913

'My grandfather, Titus Huggins, was born at Swagwater [now called Haywood] and took over Gorsley Court Farm sometime after 1913. We know that because the sale of the property for £37 10s [£37.50] to Alfred Drinkwater in 1913 is in the Onslow estate documents.

'My maternal grandfather, Charlie Pensom was a basket maker who lived at The Vee. He had been crippled when his knee cap slipped when scrumping for apples so had to earn his living basketmaking. He worked in the living room using withies from Carswells Farm, Upleadon and transported by donkey cart. If you look you can see the tether chain of the donkey is still embedded in the hedge by Brockmoor Head.

'My father, Percival Huggins, was born in 1894. When he was younger he worked getting cordwood for the ovens and pea sticks, later on he did timber tushing and of course worked on the farm. He took over the farm when he returned from the war in 1918. My mother, Phyllis Pensom, worked on the farm as well, and looked after the house of course. Before she was married she was a postwoman and worked at Kilcot Post Office'.

As a child in the 1920s and 1930s Eric Hayward remembers Frank's grandfather, Charlie Pensom, but with mixed feelings: 'Mr

Working life at the turn of the century: Roadmaking

Pensom, the basket-maker, had a donkey and cart that he drove to Newent on Saturdays to get his groceries. He would stop off at the Kilcot Inn—we had a large ring for tethering horses—and when I was a child I used to feed the donkey until one day it bit me!'

But life on the farm held few attractions for the young Frank Huggins. 'I didn't like farming and there wasn't enough money in it to keep us all'. His elder sisters had started out their working life by going into domestic service and worked variously at Linton Hall, at Lydney Park for Lord Bledisloe and as a nanny for the Rudges of Baysham. Ruby eventually became a teacher at Gorsley Goffs (see p.52). His brother Geoffrey emigrated to Australia after being in the army, but Frank was a child of the motor age and worked at Gouldings as a garage mechanic and driver. 'I'd never taken a test, I just started driving the lorries,' he explained. It was while driving one of these lorries and delivering to Gloucester Market that he met his wife, Sylvia, who worked in the offices for Spears Meat Wholesalers. Now their two sons seem to have inherited their grandfather's way with wood—Robin is a carpenter and Wayne a saw doctor.

Another driver for R.H. Goulding was Jack Smith, who helped his wife, Mary (Hayward) run the Kilcot Inn. He had served as a soldier abroad with the Royal Engineers during the Second World War and had been one of the first Allied soldiers to enter the concentration camps.

Mary's brother, Eric Hayward, was a naval officer. 'I was in the Merchant Navy from 1938 to 1948 and saw active service all over the world during the war. At the end of the war I served in the Pacific. [Eric was awarded many medals, including the Atlantic Star, the North Africa Star and the Burma Star]. After the navy I went into teaching and started off at Picklenash School and I taught PE and games at Newent School. There were a number of gypsy children at the school at this time and I got interested in their needs'. Eventually, after studying in Birmingham, Eric pursued a career in special education.

For many young men who saw active service in the War or did National Service afterwards, the opening of new horizons led them to move away from the land and sometimes away from the community. But others stayed, often drawn by family ties or a love of the land.

When Gerald Yeates was three years old his father died, at the tragically early age of 48. His mother and her five children came back to Kilcot to live with her parents who ran a poultry farm near Kilcot Cross. Gerald still lives there, although the old bungalow was replaced by a more modern house in 1987.

'When I left school at 14 I went to work at Knapp Farm, along the Aston Ingham road, where they made cider. They crushed every-

thing in together! I did all sorts of manual work round the farm, which also grew hay, corn, sugar beet, mangolds for fodder and kept sheep and cattle. I did farm work on different farms and was a tractor driver for the Land Settlement Association until my National Service.

Making wooden wheels for carts before rubber tyres were widespread

73

Cider-making at Aston Mill

'I signed on for three years with the Royal Artillery and was based in Glasgow. I can remember the smog we had in those days, but most of the time I worked as a colonel's driver all around the west of Scotland inspecting gunsites.

'When I'd finished my National Service (in 1956) I came home and worked for Weston's, delivering bread. Then I had a number of different jobs in the building trade, including working for Marley, erecting garages. I also did factory work for Bryce Berger, Armstrong Siddeley and Xerox. My last job was for Newent's Dial-a-ride for seven years.

'One of the early jobs I had was building the Permali factory. I acted as the tea boy and cooked sausages and onions on a tortoise stove and served them up in a bread roll. They cost me threepence to do and I sold 'em for sixpence. There was no job security in those days, they only had to give you two hours notice and "them as works and does their best, goes up the road with all the rest". You had three cards—Health, Annual and Bank Holiday cards—hence the saying "collect your cards"'.

Another family which moved to the area for work and accommo-dation were the Atkinsons. 'My family have lived in the area since at least 1886—I've a letter dated 1886 to my great-grandfather, Phil Davies. He had three sons, one of whom went to America, one worked as a groom and visited America and one lived all his life at the cottage at Kilcot Nurseries, recalls Peter Atkinson.

'My father lived at Botloes Green and worked as a propagator for the Land Settlement Association and we moved to Kilcot because the opportunity was here for work and somewhere to live. [The family at one stage owned more property on Kilcot Hill incuding "Hillview" and "Hillcrest". The cottage "Hillcrest" used also to encompass the current properties of "Standfast" and "Sunnybank"].

'On this site ["Hillcrest"] there was a large cider mill and press and some of the best cider in the area was brewed here by my great-grandfather's brother, James Davies. Gallons were sold to pubs in the Forest of Dean. This was from the 1880s to the end of the 1930s. James Davies had a four-wheel dray to transport the cider. This also doubled as a hearse! When my great-uncle died in 1948 there were still barrels of cider in the field next to the cottage.

'My parents were farm workers and market gardeners. To help the family income we used to pick blackberries from the hedges for sale. In the 1930s and 1940s no machinery was used for hedge-cutting so there were always plenty to be had. We also used to pick wild daffodils from Kilcot Woods to sell at Gloucester Market or by the roadside. People used to come to see the daffodils from all around, including Bristol and Birmingham.

'Before I did my National Service I worked for a fruit farmer at Baldwin's Farm, near Newent. I could have avoided National Service as I was in what they called a "reserved occupation" but I preferred not to be tied to the fruit farm and saw this as a means of escape. I did postpone my departure from May to September to help with the blackcurrant picking.

'I did my National Service with the RAF and stayed on a further three years, serving in Egypt, Cyprus and Malta. I was based in Nicosia at the time of the Suez crisis [1956] and remember refuelling aircraft night and day for two weeks.

'When I'd finished I came back to work on the family holding, growing salad crops. It was hard work—sheer drudgery in fact, working 12 to 14 hours a day, seven days a week. I wouldn't do it again'.

Not everyone worked on the land of course, even within Kilcot and Gorsley, and gradually people were embracing new skills. The catalyst for major change was the Second World War when young men left the community and work in the fields and in factories was taken over by women.

Chapter XII
Wartime

War brings change to all communities and ours is no exception. In the First World War, 'The Great War' as it was called at the time, young men left their farms and their families and travelled across Britain and Europe, many of them never having previously ventured further afield than Gloucester or Hereford. Sadly, many of them never returned. The list of those local lads who died in the First and Second World Wars is given on p.83.

Of those who did return, some decided that the agricultural life was not for them and put to work skills they had learned in the Forces. This was true of both wars, but in the Second World War the chief difference was the reliance on women to take up work in factories as well as on the land. One resident recalls: 'During the war many women from the country areas worked in munitions factories. One such lady cycled from Little Gorsley to Newent to catch a bus to Quedgley at 6.30 am, returning home at 8 pm. Her job was stencilling serial numbers on to crates, ready for transportation, never knowing what was inside any of the crates'.

Although many of the men could have remained at home being in 'reserved occupations', that is jobs which were vital to the country's war effort, like farming, haulage, forestry and mining, most volunteered for armed service.

Fortunately for those left behind there was little danger from bombing. In all of Herefordshire only ten houses were destroyed by bombs. Occasionally German planes, returning from a raid on the Midlands or on Gloucester, would drop a spare bomb as they flew over the countryside. Gerald Yeates, then a schoolboy, remembers: 'A bomb dropped in Kilcot, at Alway House, on the conservatory, and some student lodgers with Mrs Cook at Alway House, had some shrapnel as a souvenir. There was a sentry-box on Kilcot Common and it was manned at the time when the bomb was dropped but when the sentry, complete with 12-bore shot-gun, was asked the next day where it had dropped he said he didn't know. It was only down the lane opposite! The bombers flew over here on their way to the Midlands. A line of bombs was jettisoned along Knights Hill near Lea village. Mr Mills of Mount Pleasant, Kilcot, was a special constable during the war, checking the blackout'.

In August 1940 an incendiary bomb fell in Gorsley, but there is no note of any damage. The only other record of bombs falling was in October 1941 at Jays Green (by the M50 junction), but no damage was done. This was noted in the Gorsley Goffs School records, and it was at the school that the greatest changes were seen. On September 3rd 1939 the headmaster, Mr Warren, was instructed to close the school 'until further notice', but just over a week later the school reopened to accept evacuees. The school record reads:

> September 11th. School assembled and 54 children were admitted from St Benedicts Road Council Junior Mixed School, Small Heath, Birmingham. The headmaster was instructed to send the local children home until the evacuated children have been medically inspected. Mr F.W. Smaldon and Mr R.H. Rogers, both certificated teachers who came with the children, took up duty at the school. Mr Smaldon stayed at the school until May 21st 1942. Mr Rogers returned to take up duties in Birmingham. November 24th 1939. Twenty of the evacuees returned to Birmingham.

Evacuees

In the interwar years the average attendance at the school had been 55 pupils. Suddenly this was doubled by an influx of children from a major city—children who were away from their families and in a very strange environment. Little wonder that within weeks nearly half of them decided to go home. But later in the war more children would arrive, another 12 from Dixon Road Infants School in Birmingham in November 1940 and the following June, 27 children from Litherland, a suburb of Liverpool. In order to cope with this influx of pupils the school had to operate a shift system for classes. As one pupil described it, 'classes were spasmodic'. Another pupil recalls the arrival of the evacuees:

'Not long after the outbreak of war children from Liverpool and Birmingham were sent to Gorsley as evacuees. Boys and girls between the ages of six and ten arrived with their gas masks and the few possessions they could carry. Most of the villagers took in two and some had three children in their home to look after during the war years. It was thought safer for these children to be in the country as places like Liverpool, Birmingham and other large cities, were being bombed. Some of the children got very homesick and returned home after a short while, others stayed for the duration of the war, enjoying country life and have remained friends with local people ever since.

'At school it was difficult with the extra children, especially as there were only three classrooms. The largest classroom was divided into two by a large curtain, but it wasn't very satisfactory, but everyone got on with the job and seemed to manage quite well. During the war concerts were performed at the school by the Co-op Troop. The floodlights were paraffin lamps. Music lessons were given by the teacher who also put on concerts using local talent.

'One evacuee thought it would be nice to give her teacher a bunch of flowers; little did the teacher know that they had just been picked from the headmaster's garden'.

As well as the shift system for classes the war imposed its own timetable on the school. In September 1940 three events are of note in the School Record:

> A Daylight Cinema van showed sound films to children together from Linton School on behalf of the War Savings.
> Children visit Upton Bishop hop fields and pick hops for the Red Cross effort.
> All children have been issued with respirators; they are inspected by ARP Sgt Little.

Other entries record the school closing for two days for windows to be covered with a network of tape to stop glass splintering in case of air raids and, in the summer, numerous parties of children being sent to local farms to help with the harvest. The school building became an administrative centre for the distribution of ration books and also the focus for village efforts.

Despite its size the community raised a huge amount of money for the war effort. In May 1943 the school received a 'Certificate of Honour' for raising £500 for Tanks for Attack. During the same week the school raised £1,100 5s for the Victory Effort and, the record notes, 'the local Savings Group has raised more than £5,000', a figure which would be worth well over £100,000 today (2001). It is an astonishing amount for a small rural community.

'Harvest Workers' Playtime'

The efforts of the community had been awarded national recognition in September 1942 when the popular radio programme 'Workers' Playtime' was broadcast from Linton Hall in a tribute to the farm workers and all those helping to bring in the harvest. According to the *Daily Mirror* of September 17th: 'To take the concert to a rural area and perform to the farm hands was a gesture of thanks by the Ministry of Labour and the Ministry of Agriculture. And it was deserved'.

Although 'Workers' Playtime' was usually broadcast live at lunchtime three times a week, in this case the concert was held in the evening so that harvest could continue. Renamed 'Harvest Workers' Playtime' the variety concert of music, song and comedy acts, was held on a stage in the open air. 'The stage with its decorations of hops, sheaves of corn, mangolds, etc, was situated 'neath the tall fir trees lining the drive up to the hall,' reported that week's *Ross Gazette*.

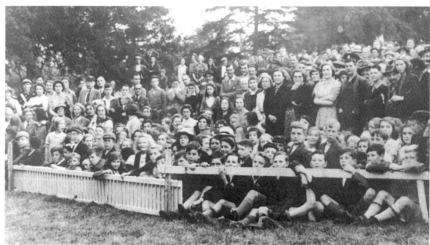

An appreciative audience for 'Harvest Workers' Playtime' at Linton Hall

Two pianos were placed on the stage and the programme began with George Myddleton and Bruce Merrill performing the air 'The English Rose'. This was followed by three songs from Patricia Burke, a leading revue singer of the time. 'Emelio the popular piano accordionist ... met with an enthusiastic reception' the *Gazette* records and then the comic duo Kenway and Young brought the house down with their interpretation of agricultural life and in particular 'Mr Pootle, the oldest inhabitant'. The show ended with community singing, as was customary during the war years and a collection was taken up for the Red Cross Fund. In 1941 the Gorsley Village fête had raised over £140 for this cause.

St Dunstan's

The St Dunstan's charity helped servicemen and women who had lost their sight and retrained many of them to new occupations. One such was Able Seaman Charles Henry Stock who was wounded in 1918. Mr Stock joined St Dunstan's in 1925 where he retrained as a mat-maker and also in poultry farming. Two years later he and his wife came to Bull Hill, Gorsley where they set up a poultry farm, later moving to bigger premises near Ross where they kept about 700 birds and also had a large number of fruit trees on their 10 acres of land. Mr and Mrs Stock moved to Southampton after the war, where he continued with poultry rearing until his death in 1961.

In Retrospect

The 'invasion' of evacuees on Gorsley Goffs School and the effect on the wartime community was recorded in a play 'Strangers in the Countryside' written by the Baptist minister, Patrick Goodland, and performed at the Chapel in 1995. Over 700 people attended the performances including several of the evacuees, who presented a plaque to the school.

As part of their history lessons children today at the school learn about what happened to their school during the Second World War. Below are a few of their impressions:

'Parents and teachers got worried and sent the children away to the countryside. Some children were evacuated here to Gorsley. Mr Chamberlain's message on the "wireless" with the words "We are currently at war with Germany" was heard by thousands all over Britain.

Children from Gorsley Goffs School re-enact the story of the evacuees

'After being evacuated the evacuees still had to go to school and as Gorsley Goffs was the nearest, coachloads of children from Birmingham and coachloads from Liverpool ended up going as well as regulars. With extra children they needed extra classrooms, Class 6 was partitioned in two by a curtain. A great advantage to this is if you sat near the curtain and found Miss Huggins boring you could pop behind and listen to Mr Warren, the headmaster. Mr Warren's nickname was Gaffer Warren'.

'Life in Gorsley 60-70 years ago was very hard but enjoyable, the war was coming and evacuees were flooding the streets, this gave children an opportunity to make friends. Children and mothers would cry and weep as the children left for the countryside. A coach load of Liverpool and Birmingham children arrived here in Gorsley. The children who originally attended the school were very happy as they had a few days off while the evacuees were being sorted. School life in Gorsley 60-70 years ago was very much the same but I think in school everybody was very lucky because they had optional home-work and no school uniform'.

'Children at school, including evacuees did not want to leave school at the end of the day because they had to help their mums at home with chores like collecting firewood or milking the cows. When the evacuees came down to Gorsley they did not know what a cow looked like'.

CHAPTER XIII
In Memoriam

The young men of our community who fell in the First and Second World Wars are remembered in the churches and chapels of Gorsley, Kilcot, Linton and Clifford's Mesne—the places where they had lived or where their families still resided.

From the records it is not always easy to tell precisely in which of these villages someone had lived. And so we commemorate them all.

William Apperley	Thomas Johnson
Frank Ballinger	Kenneth Knight
Abel Bodenham	Maurice Knight
John Dallimore	James Lewis
Henry Davis	Hubert Matthews
George Fishpool	Richard Napier
Reginald Fishpool	Norman Smith
Walter Fishpool	Wallace Sysum
Melville Gardner	Herbert Taylor
Henry Hale	William Wadley
Bernard Humpherson	Walter Webley
Alfred James	Francis Wheeler

'... Tell them of us and say,
For our tomorrows they gave their today'

Chapter XIV
The Present Generation

While the wartime experiences altered lives drastically for many, the chief agent of change for today's residents has been the coming of the M50 motorway and the increase of mobility that car ownership has brought. Not only didquiet country lanes become busy highways, but families who for generations lived, worked and played within an area of only a few miles now sought work and leisure from further afield. And by the same token Gorsley and Kilcot became the home of many people who had no previous connection with the area.

In 1984 Sarah Ferguson, aged six, moved to Kilcot, although her family had lived in the county for a dozen or so years before. Like many Kilcot children before her, Sarah attended Glebe Infants, Picklenash Junior and Newent Community Schools. Unlike those children a generation earlier, however, she went to senior school by car and when she got there could enjoy the sports facilities including a swimming pool, work on computers—as she had done at Picklenash—and take part in music and drama. And in 1986 Sarah had travelled further than most: 'For a year I attended Picnic Point Public School in Australia—a long way down under!'

Although many of her out-of-school activities were linked to the school, or to organisations like the Girl Guides, like earlier generations Sarah spent some of her time playing with her brother and sister, enjoying a game of cricket or tennis in the garden or playing indoors in bad weather.

Her near contemporary, Amanda Price, also liked music, was an enthusiastic Guider and enjoyed swimming and badminton. Amanda's family has lived in the area for three generations and she remembers playing with goats and pigs and feeding lambs when she was a little girl.

Boys seem to have different pastimes, some of which probably have not changed for more than a hundred years! 'I used to go out exploring—take a packed lunch and go out all day—all the places I shouldn't have been. I liked making things, like go-carts with wheels, and making dens too,' confesses James Crowhurst, who came to Kilcot in 1982, aged seven. His contemporary, Stephen Burson also liked to build dens, climb trees and camp out. 'And we explored old derelict cottages—there were lots derelict then!'

'Den-making' was also a favourite pastime of Winston Gooch, alongside 'football, cricket, cider drinking and badminton'. Winston's family have been in the area for over a century as farm and forestry workers. Winston would work on the family farm and also pick apples and pears for cider-making and help with haymaking as a young boy in the 1970s and 1980s. A decade on James Crowhurst would also go fruit-picking and do a bit of gardening to earn some pocket money, while Esther Howley recalls haymaking on her uncle's farm and also, in the late 1980s, 'I worked on the milk round with

The Ferguson children play on their garden swing,
as country children have done for generations

Gooch's on Saturdays for several years in my late teens'. The milk round is the one currently run by Winston Gooch.

The tradition of working on the land to help the family business or to earn a little extra money has not altered through the ages. Stephen Burson went fruit-picking to earn a bit of money and he can remember cider-making at Aston Mill, Aston Crews, with his father, Bob Gwynn and Jimmy Elsmore. Sean Burkill, now just in his thirties and whose family has lived in the area for over 100 years, remembers helping his grandparents by picking apples and perry pears and also going haymaking in Kilcot and Gorsley. Elizabeth Taylor is about ten years younger than Sean, and her family has lived in the area 'as far back as we know'. She also worked on a local fruit farm 'to earn myself money during the school holidays, picking soft fruit and apples,' and on the family farm feeding the animals, milking cows, suckling calves and picking fruit.

Sarah Hamblin helped with the family business—market gardening—by picking tomatoes, cutting lettuces and potting and planting crops. In her free time as a child in the 1960s and 1970s she enjoyed swimming (she attended Newent Community School) and looking after her pets—dogs, guinea pigs and rabbits. At school the girls still played hopscotch and skipping and in Sarah's day trousers were *not* an option for girls at Newent School. A decade on Esther Howley remembers skipping in the school playground, playing 'jacks' and different varieties of tag, and also cycling round the area.

Some traditions never die out, it seems. Hopscotch and skipping were also childhood activities of Lydia Buckley, today only in her early twenties and born and brought up in the area, although her family only moved here in the 1970s. Lydia used computers at school, but out of hours went camping, climbed trees and even built dens! And although there was now a swimming pool at Newent School, in the 1980s and 1990s Elizabeth Taylor went swimming in the brook just like countless schoolchildren born decades before her. And fished with home-made rods and built dams and played on the farm.

So is the present 'new' generation much different from their fore-bears? Only in their aspirations it would seem. For many higher education is a norm, a stepping stone to a career in the professions, something many parents and grandparents could only have dreamed of. For others the goal is to travel and see a bit of the world before settling down. Some want to or already do run their own business.

But perhaps the best summary of the ambitions of today's young people, and one which spans the generations, is that from Winston Gooch: 'To be happy and successful'.

CHAPTER XV
Fun Day

The idea of the communities of Kilcot and Gorsley getting together to celebrate the new millennium was first put forward at a Christ Church Parochial Church Council meeting in February 1998. Local people and organisations were contacted and in September fourteen representatives from village organisations attended an open meeting at the church chaired by Revd Robert Simpson, Rector of the Newent Benefice which includes Christ Church.

Agreement was quickly reached on the overall idea to have a joint celebration and various ideas were debated. Following a further meeting in November a steering group was established, with Robert Simpson as chairman and Vivien Ferguson as secretary. The group included representatives from the Church, Chapel, Gorsley Goffs School, the Gorsley Village Hall Committee, Gardening Club, WI, Parish Councils, Neighbourhood Watch groups, as well as individuals from both communities.

It was decided to hold a celebration Fun Day on Saturday May 6th 2000 at Gorsley Village Hall, to publish a book on Gorsley and Kilcot past and present, and to present a gift of a specially commissioned china mug to each child aged under 16 on December 31st 2000. The mug design was by Lyle Walker of the Art Club.

The daytime celebrations were to be followed by an evening of Forest fun and songs with well-known local entertainer Dick Brice and culminating in a grand firework display. Additionally, on the evening of Friday, May 5th, Dr Cecil H. Clough, FSA, a Gorsley resident and historian would give a talk at Gorsley Goffs School, entitled 'Gorsley over the centuries'.

A pair of commemorative mugs made for the millennium and given to each child aged under 16 on December 31st 2000

Grants and Sponsors

As the events were not planned to be profit-making, grants and sponsorship was sought to help cover the costs of the gift to the children, the cost of hired events and of publicity and advertising. In all grants totalling £1,200 were received from the Forest of Dean District Council, Newent Town Council, Linton Parish Council and Gorsley and Kilcot Parish Council. Donations totalling £285 were received from the following local businesses: Patrick Buckley of Reg Davis & Co, building contractors; Julian Cox, veterinary surgeon; Dave Crowhurst, Church Farm Guest House; Martyn Davy, chartered accountant; Mark Goulding, agricultural engineer; Nick Horniman, Pets Barn Veterinary Centre; Martyn Vick and Malcolm Jennings, Ford Farm Eggs and Holiday Lodges; Les Lane, LH Lane, Brickhouse Motors.

The Celebrations

The events started off with Dr Clough's talk on the Friday. Dr Clough very kindly gave his time and expertise free of charge and admission was by free ticket. The hall at Gorsley Goffs School was filled to over-

Face-painting at the Fun Day

flowing and the lecture which covered the history of the village up to the turn of the last century, was very well-received. A video recording of the talk and slide presentation was made by Richard Errett.

Despite a cloudy start the next morning, the weather brightened and by the time the Fun Day was officially opened by Revd Roy Chivers, team vicar and Gorsley resident, it was a hot and sunny after-noon. Every aspect and organisation of community life was repre-sented by the events, stalls and sideshows; these included a Book stall; a White Elephant stall; Craft and Cake stall run by Pound Farm and Ryelands; Plant stall run by the Gardening Club; Skittles run by Christ Church; Tombola run by Gorsley Village Hall; Face Painting run by the Toddlers Group; Coconut Shy run by the Neighbourhood Watch groups; Veterinary Advice from Pets Barn Vet Centre; Hot-dog stall run by Gorsley Baptist Chapel, who also loaned the PA and sound system; Soft Drinks stall; Tea and Cakes served by the WI; British Legion display; Lifeboat Association display and sale of goods.

To add to the fun a number of stalls were hired including the Gladiators, Crazy Bikes, Jumping Frogs, Hook a Duck, Milk the Cow,

Fun Day skittles

Mr Sunshine entertains the children

Plants for sale: one of the many well-patronised stalls

and Jumbo Buzz. There was also a Balloon Race (organised by Doug
Swallow), Antiques Quiz (organised by Daphne Toner), Trivia Quiz
(organised by Jenny Carling), an exhibition by the Art Club and an
exhibition of photos of Gorsley and Kilcot at the present time
(organised by Gloria Pay).

The younger ones were kept enthralled by Mr Sunshine, the
much-loved local children's entertainer, and as the afternoon wore
on the ice-cream van was very well patronised and the hot-dog stall-
holders sweated! First Aid cover was provided by Daphne Toner of
the St John's Ambulance Association. Norman Gooch lent his field
for car-parking, which was organised by Richard Goulding and
Duncan Charles. The teas and cakes served in the hall were accom-
panied by excellent music from a wind ensemble with Patrick
Buckley and friends.

The afternoon was well attended by Gorsley and Kilcot residents
past and present and the day was a great success and amply rewarded
all the hard work and preparation. It was a true community event—
and it wasn't over. In the Gorsley Village Hall the evening of Forest

songs and anecdotes with Dick Brice from The Lea, was a sell-out. A bar was provided for the evening with Richard Errett and his son, Matthew, working hard behind the scenes and Sue and Ron Upward continuing their hard work of the afternoon selling hot dogs. The evening was a great success, finishing off with an excellent firework display at about 11 pm, with Revd Robert Simpson and Martyn Davy setting off the pyrotechnics!

The final part of the planned celebrations for the Millennium is this book. The basis for it is the research undertaken by Eileen Chivers who interviewed many of the residents whose memories stretch back fifty years or more. Eileen also collected together archive material and many of the photographs of times past. Such has been the interest shown in the project that it has grown to go back further in time and also to come right up to the present with the formation of the new parish council and the results of our community appraisal. It is hoped that it will be a lasting reminder of our communities for years to come.

Chapter XVI
Into the New Millennium

The Year 2000 was a landmark for everyone, but it had an especial place in the lives of the people of Gorsley and Kilcot. In April of that year, after months of campaigning, it became the newest civil parish in the county of Gloucestershire. (That part of Gorsley which comes under Herefordshire County Council is part of a parish council with Linton.)

Until then the civil (as opposed to the ecclesiastical) parish administration had been part of Newent Town. At the District Council level (the next one up) Gorsley and Kilcot was part of the Newent and Oxenhall ward. While there was no question that residents did not feel part of Newent—it is the nearest shopping centre, most services, like doctor, dentist and police are based in the town—there was a growing feeling that the Town Council of Newent did not recognise the needs of this rural area. Matters came to a head when the co-ordinator of the new Gorsley local Neighbourhood Watch committee, Judy Sleet, asked for some Watch signs to be put up in the village. The request was refused, even though the cost was only a few hundred pounds and the total council tax paid to the town council came to about £4,000 a year.

The campaign started and Judy Sleet and district councillor Martyn Vick organised a referendum on becoming a separate civil parish. The overwhelming 'yes' response was a major reason why the Secretary of State agreed to the request. Elections were held in March 2000 and seven councillors elected from a field of twelve candidates. The first councillors were: Judy Sleet (Chair), Molly Boughton, Dave Crowhurst, Viv Ferguson, Graham Price, Pat Scott and Martyn Vick.

*Gorsley & Kilcot Parish Councillors, from left to right
(standing): Graham Price, Molly Boughton, Pat Scott, Dave Crowhurst;
(seated): Martyn Vick, Judy Sleet, Viv Ferguson*

It was with a great sense of achievement that the New Millennium was celebrated with a 'Fun Day' on May 6th 2000. The plans for this, and other celebrations, had been started back in February 1998 at a meeting of the Parochial Church Council held at Christ Church (see p.89). The initial decision then, to unite the communities of Kilcot and Gorsley for events to mark the millennium, played a major part in motivating the community to have its own civil parish council.

The Way Ahead
In September 2000 a well-attended Gorsley & Kilcot parish meeting agreed that it would be useful to carry out an appraisal to find out in

more detail what residents wanted—and didn't want—and how they thought the parish should develop. With the help of a computer program developed at the Countryside and Community Research Unit at Cheltenham and Gloucester College of Higher Education, a questionnaire was devised and distributed in February 2001. A response rate of just over 80% was achieved.

This snapshot of the community in the early spring of 2001 revealed:

- Almost one third of residents are aged between 45 and 60.
- One in 12 are children of school age, and a similar percentage are people over 85.
- About half are in employment and for 68% of them a car or van is the way they get to work.
- One in 10 run their own business, but one third of these are 'professional services' and only one in five is in agriculture or horticulture. Almost all of the self-employed work on their own or employ one or two people at most.

And what do people want most? The overwhelming response is to do with the roads: better maintenance; more speed restrictions and

Agriculture still has its place in the community. 'Tickle' a Gloucester Old Spot sow belonging to the Kilcot Herd of Mr & Mrs S.L. Barnfield, was awarded the title Champion of Champions in July 2000 following the Royal Show

Gorsley Goffs school photo, Summer 2001

traffic calming; improved pavements and cycle paths and better signage, especially road names.

For all our reliance on cars for work and leisure most parishioners still find time to go for a walk in the countryside and enjoy its beauty. About one-third of residents were born here or have lived here for at least 25 years, but of the reasons for moving to the area over half enthusiastically replied that they came to Gorsley and Kilcot because of a love of country life. The comments of one resident (whether an incomer or born here is not known) sums up many people's views: 'We are lucky to live in a beautiful area that should have access for all. But don't allow it to become a weekend/holiday home village. Agriculture should not be overtaken by tourists. We can all share the countryside but we must protect it and look after it for future generations'.

The next century
And what about the future generations? Some of the final year pupils (aged 10 or 11) at Gorsley Goffs School described their life today and ambitions for the future.

(Trahearne Portraits)

'I am a 10-year-old girl at Gorsley Goffs Primary School ... I have a mum, a dad and two sisters. I've just arrived home after a summer holiday in Looe. Also the week before last Class 6 went for a trip to Wales, in the Rhondda Valley. We explored many mountains and coal mines. We looked at many museums and found out about the past'. (Harriet Baynham-Williams)

'My name is Lauren Brandon and I'm 11 years old. My dad is Welsh and my mum is half Spanish and half English. So because of that when I was 10 I had to start Spanish classes. When I'm older my ambitions are to be a model and open up my own business as a fashion designer. I also want to get married in the Dominican Republic and have a villa in Spain. As well as that I want to have kids. Whether my dreams come true we'll just have to wait and see'. (Lauren Brandon)

'I am reaching the end of my time at Gorsley Goffs Primary School. I have many friends at this school and I'll hate it when I have to say goodbye to them because I will miss them very much. There are many clubs like music, hockey, art, netball, cricket. My best subject is art. So I could say I've had the best time at Gorsley Goffs Primary School'. (Charlotte Wilband)

'My name is Isabel Juliet Neal Hooke but my friends call me Issy. I was born a twin with my sister Lucinda, I'm older by one minute so I was first to walk and talk. My favourite subject is games because I like going to the district sports. After school I go to netball, rounders and cricket club. At the weekend I go riding for an hour ... I'd like a pony of my own but for now I have two ducks, one cat, one horse, two rabbits and nineteen chickens. In my life I would like to work with animals or do something with music as I play the piano and have passed grade 1 with distinction'. (Isabel Hooke)

'I'm Lucy and I have a sister named Isabel. She is my twin. Being a twin can sometimes be annoying but mostly it's OK. My hobbies are horse riding (I have recently galloped) as well as playing tennis. My favourite thing to do apart from riding is looking after animals. I have chickens (all with personalities) two friendly ducks, one very naughty rabbit (and another one to keep it company) a cat and my mum has a show horse. I eventually want to get a proper pony of my own as well as a dog. My ambitions are to become a TV presenter (hopefully become rich) then when I have retired I hope to become a famous horse rider'. (Lucy Hooke)

'My name is Elizabeth Amy Birtles and I live at Hundred House in Botloes Green. I have a mum, a dad, a brother, a sister and a very mental dog called Tucker who is an Australian Shepherd. We moved to Hundred House about five or six years ago. Our garden altogether has nine and a half acres of land, including two big fields and two little gardens at the side of the house and in the first little garden we have a big trampoline which is about two metres by one metre.

School so far is quite interesting as we've just got a new teacher called Mr Horsburgh and I'm going on my second residential to Wales; the SATs are coming up next week which I am quite worried about, but thankfully I've got some booklets about them to help me.

When I grow up I hope to become a primary school teacher and for my family to be happy'. (Elizabeth Birtles)

'My life so far has been a dream. I've got all the things a child could want. My Mum and Dad have been the best, not only do they look after and care for their own four children but they share their love and affection with other children who aren't as fortunate as us, as they are approved respite foster carers. My ambitions for the future are to become a teacher or a singer. My biggest hope is that the world will become a better place with less pollution for people of the future'. (Amber Williams)

What more appropriate way to end this book than with a child's hope for a better world—a hope that has surely been shared by those who have lived here throughout the ages.

Select Bibliography

Bick, David, *The Mines of Newent and Ross* (The Pound House, Newent, 1987)

Burke, Thomas, *Travel in England* (Batsford, 1942)

Dohar, William J, *The Black Death and Pastoral Leadership: The Diocese of Hereford in the Fourteenth Century* (University of Pennsylvania Press, 1995)

Finberg, H.P.R., 'The Making of the English Landscape', *The Gloucestershire Landscape* (Hodder, 1975)

Goodland, Revd Patrick, The Gorsley Chapel Story (in press)

Hart, Cyril, *The Verderers and Forest Laws of Dean* (David & Charles, 1971)

Herbert, Nicholas, *Road Travel and Transport in Gloucestershire* (Gloucester County Library and Alan Sutton, 1985)

Hurley, Heather, *The Old Roads of South Herefordshire* (The Pound House, Newent 1992)

Hurley, Heather, *The Story of Ross* (Logaston Press, 1999)

Newent Town Guide (Newent Civic Society, 2001)

Pereira, W.D., *The Siege of Gloucester* (Stoate and Bishop, 1983)

Porter, Stephen, *Destruction in the English Civil War* (Sutton Publishing, 1994)

Verey, David, *Buildings of England, Gloucestershire: The Vale and Forest of Dean*, (Penguin, 1975)

Zeigler, Philip, *The Black Death* (Sutton Publishing, 1969)

Additionally, of course, I consulted a number of standard texts and reference books to confirm names, dates and places and also delved into leaflets and booklets on local buildings, museums and collections for further information.

The spelling of place names follows the Ordnance Survey Pathfinder series of 1994 unless used in quotation, when archaic spellings may be found.